THE
GODFATHER
A PICTORIAL HISTORY
MOVIES

THE
GODFATHER
A PICTORIAL HISTORY
MOVIES

Gerald Gardner & Harriet Modell Gardner

WINGS BOOKS

NEW YORK ■ AVENEL, NEW JERSEY

This 1993 edition is published by Wings Books,
distributed by Outlet Book Company, Inc., a Random House Company,
40 Engelhard Avenue, Avenel, New Jersey 07001.

ACKNOWLEDGMENTS

We are indebted to the files of the Margaret Herrick Library of the Academy of Motion
Picture Arts and Sciences. For their help in collecting the photos in this book, we
gratefully acknowledge the assistance of Larry Edmunds Bookstore, Movie Star News,
Cinemabilia, The Memory Shop, Motion Picture T.V. Photo Archive, and the Museum
of Modern Art Photo Archive. Other stills are from the authors' own collection. The
movie stills are courtesy of Paramount Pictures, Columbia, MGM, 20th Century Fox,
Universal, Warner Bros., Walt Disney Co., Tri-Star, Orion, and United Artists. Special
thanks to Paramount Pictures which produced and distributed the *Godfather* movies, for
the use of production stills from these films. Other photos are courtesy of the White
House, The Smithsonian Institute, The National Archives, United Press International, and
the presidential libraries of John F. Kennedy, and Lyndon B. Johnson. The three
Godfather films are now available in a deluxe boxed video edition, *The Godfather Trilogy.*

Random House
New York · Toronto · London · Sydney · Auckland

Printed and bound in the United States of America

Library of Congress Cataloging-in-Publication Data

Gardner, Gerald C.
    The Godfather movies : a pictorial history / Gerald Gardner and
Harriet Modell Gardner.
        p.   cm.
    Includes bibliographical references.
    ISBN 0-517-07372-2
    1. Godfather (Motion picture)   2. Godfather, part II.
3. Godfather, part III.   I. Gardner, Harriet Modell.   II. Title.
PN1997.G56833G37   1993
791.43′72—dc20   92-34866
                                                              CIP

8   7   6   5   4   3   2   1

to Nestle Modell
with sincerest love

to Emanuel Modell
with warmest memories

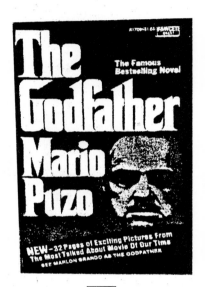

CONTENTS CONTENTS

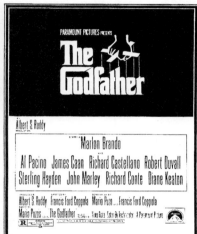

THE WALL STREET JOURNAL.

Los Angeles Times

THE NEW REPUBLIC

Newsweek

Esquire   New York

7

CONTENTS CONTENTS CONTENTS

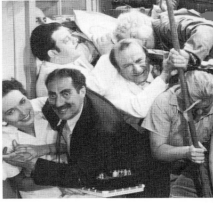

CONTENTSCONTENTS

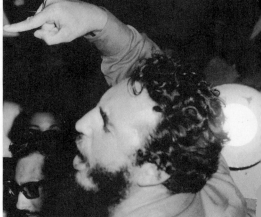

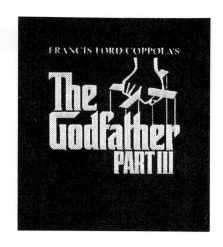

FRANCIS FORD COPPOLA'S
The Godfather PART III

CONTENTS CONTENTS

It would be no exaggeration to call *The Godfather* an Italian-American *Gone With the Wind*. It raised the crime film to an affecting new intensity. Before *The Godfather*, most gangster movies focused on the killings and the car chases, the bullets and the bombs. These films thrived on action and were scant on insight. As with *The French Connection* and *Bullitt*, the ones that were shrewd in their depiction of violence were most popular. But Francis Ford Coppola widened the scope. He peered into the motives of the criminal mind and the soul of its society.

The Godfather and its two superlative sequels reached new heights. Of course, these films contain many violent episodes. Indeed, to prevent the audience becoming bored by the numerous killings, Coppola is careful to make each one exceedingly clever. But the director does not merely exploit murder; he explores people. Particularly in the first film, Coppola examines the motives of his individuals with as much care as would playwrights such as Arthur Miller or Tennessee Williams. But in the case of *The Godfather*, the characters have a nasty predilection for murder.

Characters claim repeatedly that the killings are not motivated by anger; as the hot-headed Sonny insists, "It's business, it's not personal." Nonetheless, the killings and the insights into character go hand-in-hand. The malignancy of murder, as practiced by the Corleones, may be a metaphor for aggressive ambitions within modern society. In fact, some solemn sociologists state that the *Godfather* films are an exposé on capitalism and the American way of life. One can view *Citizen Kane* as an examination of yellow journalism and *Gone With the Wind* as a study of assertive versus passive people, or one can simply accept them as sparkling entertainment. So it is with *The Godfather*. Whether or not one adopts the sociologists' view, the *Godfather* movies are absolutely riveting. And whether the film is a metaphor or a spanking good story, it holds the audience in its breathtaking grip.

━━━━━

The *Godfather* movies are a marvelous and surprising achievement for several reasons. Gangster films have always been dubious investments. Francis Ford Coppola's films had never been known to make money. Marlon Brando was an actor whose career was in decline and who often busted budgets and enraged directors. Al Pacino was unknown, short, and looked "too Italian." The problems went on and on. But through the genius of Francis Ford Coppola, *The Godfather* changed everything. The grosses brought a king's ransom to the Paramount treasury, audiences raved, critics rhapsodized, Oscars descended, and history was made.

The *Godfather* films are unusual works of art. They provided immense financial prosperity and provoked critical applause. The movies earned Paramount $800 million, nine Oscars, and an enduring niche in our culture. Although an extraordinary thing to say about "mere movies," the *Godfather* films opened up unspeakably important facets of American life.

CHAPTER 1

The Search for a Director

WHAT ARE THE FIVE MOST popular films America has produced? Well, there's *Gone With the Wind, Citizen Kane, Casablanca, The Wizard of Oz,* and certainly *The Godfather. . . . The Godfather* made more money than all the rest, and has been described as monumental, extraordinary, incredible. Yet to Paramount Pictures it was "a quickie." And after the top brass selected brash Al Ruddy, an architect turned movie producer, to produce it, they faced the task of choosing a director.

Twenty years earlier, their big decision would have been selecting the producer, but by the early Sixties, the director was the thing. And because Paramount had lost a good deal of money over the past season and wanted to invest a modest two million dollars in *The Godfather,* they wanted a director who was a manageable, malleable fellow who would take orders, respect the budget, and be vulnerable to the influence of the front office. Boy, did they get the wrong number!

Choosing the *Godfather* director was a classic case of making the right decision for the wrong reasons. When you discover that Zero Mostel was the twelfth choice to star in *A Funny Thing Happened on the Way to the Forum,* you marvel that they didn't see he was the ideal casting in the first place. And when you hear that Francis Ford Coppola was the thirteenth choice to direct *The Godfather* you wonder why this choice was not self-evident. There must be a guardian angel who watches over the decisions of Hollywood executives.

The Paramount brass chose Coppola after twelve other directors had turned down the project. They also chose him because they thought he was eager for a project after making a few films that were far from blockbusters. They thought he would film quickly and keep his costs down. After all, two million dollars is not a lot to spend on a theatrical film; television movies are cranked out for a million and change.

But Al Ruddy and Bob Evans, production chief of Paramount, first offered *The*

Peter Yates had directed Steve McQueen in *Bullitt.* He was offered the chance to direct *The Godfather* but passed.

Costa-Gavras directed the indictment of totalitarian regimes in the political thriller *Z*, starring Yves Montand.

Costa-Gavras passed on *The Godfather*. He liked the indictment of capitalism but felt the film was "too American."

Godfather to Peter Yates, director of the crackling crime film, *Bullitt*. When he said "pass," they turned to Constantin Costa-Gavras, who had made a thrilling indictment of totalitarian regimes in *Z*. He liked the implied indictment of capitalism in the movie, but still said no because *The Godfather* was "too American." They offered it to Arthur Penn, who had brought the bloody adventures of *Bonnie and Clyde* to the screen, but he was otherwise occupied. They offered it to Franklin Schaffner, who had dealt with violence in *Planet of the Apes*, but he felt the novel was too flattering to the Mafia. They offered it to Fred Zinnemann, who had dealt with lawlessness out west in *High Noon*, but he too passed. They offered it to Richard Brooks, whose *In Cold Blood* had painted two portraits in criminal viciousness. But Brooks said no, just as he would years later when they asked him to create a sequel to the film.

Plenty of indicators showed that Coppola might be the man who could extract the most from Mario Puzo's bestselling novel. Those at Paramount who were interested in someone whose goal would be to stay under budget could recall *Finian's Rainbow*, the musical Coppola had directed for Warner Brothers for a mere three million dollars. Making a Hollywood musical for that kind of money was like making a movie on a credit card. Three million dollars was nothing when compared to the budget for contemporaneous musicals like *Funny Girl*.

Coppola was also an able scenarist whose screenplay for *Patton* showed promise of copping an Oscar, which it did. Perhaps Coppola's best qualification was that he was Italian. He seemed to understand this strange species of ethnic gangsters, the way they spoke, the way they ate, the way they treated their wives, their dynamics of loyalty and memory and vengeance. Anyone who had seen Coppola's earlier film, *The Rain People*, recalled the flashbacks to the Italian wedding, which were among the most moving scenes in the movie. Soon, another Italian wedding would become world-famous.

Coppola was not coy. He had an intuitive sense about how to make the film. In part, his urge was created by the serendipity that can govern the behavior of brilliant people: the hunch that with attention and inspiration, he could turn the book into gold. In addition,

The budget for *Funny Girl* dwarfed that of *Finian's Rainbow*, which Coppola directed on a shoestring.

Clint Eastwood and Lee Marvin in *Paint Your Wagon* started with a budget of $9 million and went to $26 million and left Paramount short on resources for *The Godfather*'s budget.

The Molly Maguires starred Sean Connery. It flopped, leading Paramount to exercise financial prudence.

he was deeply in debt. Warner Brothers had bankrolled his Zoetrope Studio, and had just pulled the plug. He owed them $600,000. Against this backdrop, Coppola showed amazing energy and ingenuity when he contrived to double his budget in order to shoot the film in a period setting and hire the stars he wanted. He placed his unmistakable imprint on the entire conception of the film, even without the clout that someone like Stephen Spielberg might possess.

Though it was a time of heavy losses for the studio, Coppola captured an increased commitment and investment. Paramount had endured a string of failures that filled the air with the smell of burning money. *Catch-22*'s budget had ballooned from ten to twenty-four million dollars. The budget for *Paint Your Wagon,* in which Clint Eastwood sang "Wand'ring Star" while music critics winced, had started at nine and soared to twenty-six million dollars. *Darling Lili* and *The Molly Maguires* had flopped. *Those Daring Young Men in Their Jaunty Jalopies* had gone down in flames. Paramount could not afford another daring young man

Stanley Jaffe, Paramount's president, had been executive producer of *Goodbye, Columbus,* starring Richard Benjamin.

with a jaunty attitude toward the budget. They wanted Coppola to make his movie quickly and inexpensively.

But Paramount did not bargain for Coppola's powers of persuasion. Al Ruddy should have known what a whirlwind he was riding. He himself was a superior salesman who had sold and produced four entertaining movies, aimed at young moviegoers, which all proved anemic at the box office. But he had also created a successful television sitcom in *Hogan's Heroes* and cast it adroitly. Ruddy arranged a meeting for Coppola with Bob Evans, Peter Bart, the studio executive who had optioned Puzo's book, and Stanley Jaffe, Paramount's president (who had been executive producer of *Goodbye Columbus,* the successful film based on the work by Philip Roth).

In briefing Coppola for the meeting, Ruddy underlined the major point to stress. If Coppola wanted to be offered the movie, he must remember that Paramount wanted a two-million-dollar movie, period. End of paragraph. But at the meeting, the incandescent Coppola ignored the script that had been written for him by Ruddy. He launched into an inspirational speech on his own theory of moviemaking. By all accounts, it was a sparkling display of salesmanship and flamboyance. At one point he jumped on the desk for emphasis. Paramount was sold. Coppola got *The Godfather.*

Despite his weak bargaining position, Coppola's deal with Paramount wasn't all bad. Attorney Norman Garey (who a few years later would shock the Hollywood community by taking his own life) made a deal that gave Coppola a modest $150,000 to co-write and direct the film, but promised him 7.5 percent of the net profits. Of course, net profits can often be elusive in Hollywood, and unless *The Godfather* was a gargantuan hit, his percentage would be as meaningless as rain on the ocean. However, if the film were successful—no one anticipated what a great success it would be—it could bring Coppola a sizable sum. He could then devote himself to making the sort of movie he *really* preferred and he could pay off the loan on his studio.

And so the thirty-one-year-old director set about making the film something very special. George Lucas, his partner in the Zoetrope Studio, urged him to accept the offer. "Go, ahead, Francis," he said. "What have you got to lose?"

CHAPTER 2

Choosing the Don

MARLON BRANDO HAD been surrounded by plenty of violent struggles—on the docks in *On the Waterfront,* on the decks in *Mutiny on the Bounty,* in a New Orleans tenement in *A Streetcar Named Desire.* But they didn't compare to the struggles that surrounded Francis Coppola's proposal that Brando was the only man to play the Godfather.

The Paramount brass had a fit. In their eyes, Brando's career was behind him. He had a reputation as a troublemaker and a budget-breaker. In his last three movies, *Burn!, The Night of the Following Day,* and *Candy,* his disputes with directors had sent the budgets soaring. His eccentric behavior on *Mutiny on the Bounty* had created headlines in supermarket tabloids. Studio president Jaffe forbade Coppola from even *talking* about the idea of Brando as the Don, and production chief Bob Evans swore he'd rather leave Paramount than see Brando in the film. But Coppola, with the heroic obstinacy of the artist, kept lobbying for his man.

Coppola initially acquiesced to studio wishes and screen-tested virtually every older Italian actor in Hollywood, and some who were not Italian. Richard Conte and Robert Marley (who both ended up with smaller roles in the film)

were tested. Many fine actors, including Ernest Borgnine, Lee J. Cobb, Anthony Quinn, Raf Vallone, and George C. Scott, were considered. But Coppola finally reached the

George C. Scott was among the actors initially considered for the role of Don Corleone.

conclusion that natural origin had nothing to do with it. Very simply, the Godfather should be played by the best actor there is. This sharply reduced the list. It brought two names immediately to mind: Laurence Olivier and Marlon Brando. And since Olivier was ailing, it left only one. But that one set off a violent reaction in the executive suite at Paramount Pictures. Marlon Brando? Was the young director deranged?

But the director, who had been hired in part for his fancied malleability, was proving quite intractable on this point. And the starting date for production was drawing uncomfortably near. The studio asked for other casting suggestions and Coppola refused to submit any. It was Brando or bust.

An emergency meeting was convened, with high-priced lawyers scurrying about. Stanley Jaffe told Coppola he didn't want to hear another word on the subject of Brando. The director asked if he could have just five minutes to sum up the reasons for his obstinacy on the Brando nomination. Jaffe accorded him that privilege and then settled back to eye his wristwatch. But a strange thing happened. Something

out of a screenplay you might say, if you have a taste for irony. Coppola used his five minutes for a spirited speech on the reasons why Brando was really the only conceivable actor for the job.

Among Coppola's arguments was the fact that Brando, given the awe in which other actors held him, would create the "family" relationship that was essential to the atmosphere of the film. (That was indeed what happened, once production began.) Coppola reasoned, pleaded, ranted, and cajoled. What a great evangelist he would have made. He even used a device he had not resorted to since he fought for his projects at UCLA film school: at a climactic point in his monologue, he gripped his chest, fell to the floor, and feigned a seizure. Coppola's powers of persuasion won the day.

Or did they? Jaffe agreed to offer the role to Brando. But with three conditions that were virtually unfulfillable. Brando must agree to a screen test, and everyone knew that Brando never tested. He probably hadn't tested for anything since he played the son in *I Remember Mama*. Brando must agree to reimburse Paramount for any budget costs that resulted from his

behavior. And Brando must do the role for nothing, settling for a share of the profits. That Coppola managed to finesse the studio and Brando on these points is a tribute to his single-minded devotion to his vision.

Coppola had wanted Brando for the lead in another film of his, a paranoid movie called *The Conversation.* When Brando passed on the role, Coppola was shaken. But the role of Don Corleone was more to Brando's liking. He read the novel in a gulp and called the part "delicious." But Brando told the media another story: He needed the money and hadn't worked for years. (Brando has sometimes worked under the spur of necessity. Recently he took a role in the film *The Freshman,* ostensibly to help pay for the legal costs of his son Christian and the medical costs of his daughter.) Whatever the truth about Brando's motivation for playing *The Godfather,* he welcomed the role. Perhaps, like Coppola, he saw the vast potential of a movie that Paramount viewed as a low-budget gangster flick.

Brando had no illusions about his acceptability to the studios. He told Mario Puzo,

Coppola felt the Godfather should be played by the best actor in the world. This shortened the list to Olivier and Brando.

the author of *The Godfather,* that only a strong director could get Paramount to accept him. Coppola's position was not strong, but, as the saying goes, "One man with courage makes a majority." Coppola compensated for his lack of clout by being adroit and stubborn and, as it turned out, absolutely right.

The proviso of a screen test had to be squarely faced by the young director. There is a saying "When the going gets tough, the tough get going." Coppola got going.

He told Brando he would like to "explore" the role with him. Brando agreed. Coppola suggested that he videotape Brando to help get the feel of it. When the director appeared at Brando's home with a borrowed camcorder, feeling distinctly uneasy, Brando greeted him in a kimono and a ponytail. They talked about how the 47-year-old actor might play the 65-year-old Mafia chief. The Don was a magnificent old warrior, a noble killer, with a massive head, a battered face, a twisted mouth, and pugnacious jaw. Brando smeared some shoe polish on his hair, stuffed some Kleenex in his cheeks, and let his voice assume the raspy tone of a combative old man. Coppola started taping. Then suddenly a man appeared, crossed to Brando, and began to recount how boys had brutalized his daughter. Coppola had brought along an Italian barber to play the role of Bonasera, the undertaker in the opening scene of the film. He had ordered the man to wait outside Brando's home, to be summoned at a propitious moment. His ploy worked. At first, Brando was mystified by this stranger in a dark suit telling him about his daughter. But then he fell into the scene. The tape was running and Coppola had his test scene.

When Coppola showed the "screen test" to the Paramount execs, Evans and Jaffe were delighted. Evidently, Coppola had gotten over his Brando obsession and looked elsewhere. But who the devil was this guy? He was *good*. The Mafia patriarch on the screen was unsettling. His mumbled reading was seductive and improvisational. The cracked voice and clenched teeth carried menace. Here was a Don who was a primitive monster, a man who carried ancient hatreds and remembered grudges. When they realized the actor was Marlon Brando—Good Lord, it was him!—the objections to the actor evaporated. Marlon Brando was Don Corleone and Don Corleone was Marlon Brando.

Paramount President Jaffe told Coppola he didn't want to hear another word about Marlon Brando playing the Godfather.

CHAPTER 3

Casting Wars

T HE CONSTANT FRICTION and abrasions caused by sand in the oyster create the pearl. Perhaps the constant friction and abrasions in the creation of *The Godfather* formed this pearl of a movie.

In his play *The Best Man,* Gore Vidal writes an exchange between politicians that reflects the difficulty of Coppola's position:

"Nothing's easy, is it?"

"Nothing good."

Recognizing the inevitability of conflict, Coppola fought hard and won most of his contests with the front office, the producer, and the novelist.

Francis Coppola came close to being fired on no less than five occasions: when he battled for Brando; when Paramount saw the early dailies; when Coppola insisted on filming in Sicily; when he started to go well over budget; and when he defended his three-hour cut. Coppola also fought to film in New York and to set the movie in the 1940s.

Foremost among his struggles was his fight to cast the actors he wanted in many of the key roles.

Producer Ruddy saw Robert Redford in the role of Michael. He had played a Gentile college boy in *The Way We Were.*

Coppola knew that casting could make or break his film and he was ready to go to the mat. When Brando arrived at the production site and found Coppola anxious, intense, and on the edge of rage, he said, "Don't get so upset, Francis. . . . It's just a movie." Perhaps Coppola should have taken Brando's advice. But Coppola could not afford to be so philosophical. He wanted to create his vision.

In retrospect, Al Pacino seems the perfect choice for Michael, the youngest son, an Ivy League student and a war veteran who returns to the front lines of the Mafia wars. But Paramount, Al Ruddy, and Mario Puzo had other ideas.

Bob Evans wanted a major white-bread star like Ryan O'Neill in the role of Michael to bring in the heartland audience.

Warren Beatty was another major white-bread star who was considered for the pivotal role of Michael Corleone.

Producer Ruddy visualized Robert Redford in the role of Michael. Redford had played the WASPish college boy in *The Way We Were,* and Barbra Streisand, as the campus radical, had said to him: "Can I ask you a personal question? Do you smile all the time?" To lure the romantic star to the role of Michael, Ruddy directed Mario Puzo to start the screenplay with a love scene between Michael and Kay. Puzo ground his teeth and complied. The studio made Redford an offer that he found he could refuse. An offer was also made to Warren Beatty, but he too said no. He did not play an ethnic type till years later in *Bugsy*. Rod Steiger sent word that he would like to play Michael, but the actor who had been so riveting opposite Brando in *On the Waterfront* was by now too far past his prime for the role of the youthful Michael.

Meanwhile, back in the executive suite, Bob Evans had his own ideas about the best actor to play Michael Corleone. He wanted a

Bob Evans considered Jack Nicholson for the role of Michael Corleone, feeling he would not have a limiting ethnic look.

major white-bread star who could bring in the heartland audience. He cast his vote for Ryan O'Neal, who had just had a great success as the WASP Ivy Leaguer in *Love Story*. Another Bob Evans suggestion, meant to make Michael a hero without the limited appeal of an ethnic look, was Jack Nicholson. Like O'Neal, Nicholson was a star.

The ABP List (anyone but Pacino) went on. There were votes for David Carradine, Martin Sheen, Dean Stockwell, Tony LoBianco (at least the last named was Italian—how did he get on the list?). Another suggestion for the Michael role was James Caan who tested for the role, but not very well. Though Coppola did fifteen takes, Caan proved nervous and kept blowing his lines. Perhaps there would be something else for him in the film. . . . Charles Bluhdorn, Paramount's chairman, entered the chase. He suggested Charles Bronson. Was it a death wish?

But the director had seen a test that impressed him tremendously. It had been done for another film by an obscure 31-year-old New York actor named Al Pacino. At that point in his career, Pacino's only important film role was the dope addict in

For the role of Michael Corleone, Coppola fought for Al Pacino, an obscure 31-year-old New York actor. The studio said he was too Italian, too short, and tested badly.

Panic in Needle Park, a grim movie written by John Gregory Dunne and his wife, Joan Didion. But Paramount was against Pacino from the word go. There was a long list of complaints:

1. Pacino looked too Italian.
2. Pacino was too short. (Bob Evans called him "that midget Pacino.")
3. Pacino tested badly.
4. Pacino forgot his lines in the test and improvised others.
5. Pacino was not a famous actor and had scant name recognition.

When Coppola lobbied for Pacino to the growing chorus of nay-sayers, Paramount insisted the actor return for another screen test; then another; and still another—at what cost to the actor's confidence and self-esteem can only be imagined. Meanwhile, the execs made clear their distaste for Pacino by ordering the director to find thirty other actors and test them all. So Coppola, with the production's start date approaching, had to take the time from needed preproduction and devote it to shooting dozens of tests for Michael.

At this point, Coppola feared for his job on the casting of Michael Corleone. But feeling the role was

Audiences felt that Johnny Fontane was actually the young Frank Sinatra whose story it resembled. Sinatra had sung with the Tommy Dorsey band and starred in the career-making film *From Here to Eternity.*

critical to the film's success, he stood by his guns. Only Pacino would do, just as before him, only Brando would do. Finally Paramount blinked. It was said that they bowed more to the calendar than Coppola. The Puzo novel had become a smashing bestseller and they wanted the film out in time to cash in on its success. They feared that firing Coppola would cost them six months. Whatever the studio's reasoning, Coppola prevailed, and despite Pacino's ethnicity, his height, his nerves, his flubbed lines, his lame improvisations, his

lack of fame, and his absence of heartland appeal, he got the role of Michael. The rest is history. Pacino flowered in *The Godfather,* made its sequel a triumph, and dominated the third film. He also developed a separate robust screen career. Who says that Hollywood happy endings are confined to Hollywood movies?

According to Hollywood mythology, the studio is always saved from its follies by the omniscience of directors, who are the repository of all brilliance. Not so with the role of Johnny Fontane, the Don's godson, whose singing career is revitalized through the powerful influence of the Godfather. Coppola wanted a substantial singing star for the role so it would look authentic. He talked of Eddie Fisher, Vic Damone, Frankie Avalon, and Bobby Vinton. Even Frank Sinatra, Jr., got an offer, which would have had a nice resonance, since his father was the prototype of the fictional character. (Young Frank soon withdrew and wags smirked that he had heard from Old Blue Eyes, who bitterly resented the novel.) At one point Vic Damone had the role, but he too withdrew, declaring indignantly that the film reflected badly on the Italian-American people. Cynics

Scarecrow (1973)

In choosing Al Pacino for the role of Michael Corleone, director Coppola launched a thriving career that included these films.

Scarface (1983) with Michelle Pfeiffer

Serpico (1973)

Dog Day Afternoon (1975)

Bobby Deerfield (1977) with Marthe Keller

Revolution (1985)

observed that in reality, Damone felt the role was too small and the money was too little, which he ultimately conceded to be the real reasons he pulled out. The studio pressed for Al Martino. He too was a vocalist and nightclub performer, and he acquitted himself well in *The Godfather* and its sequel.

Another example of the sagacity of the Paramount front office could be found in the felicitous casting of Talia Shire to play Connie Corleone, the Don's daughter. Coppola was considering Brenda Vaccaro, Penny Marshall, Maria Tucci, Julie Gregg, and Kathleen Widdoes. Talia Shire, who is Coppola's sister, was given the part by Bob Evans while Coppola was out of the country. Coppola was furious that his sister had accepted the role without checking with him.

According to Talia, he feared that she might "fall on her face." "Just because you're a genius doesn't mean that you're completely developed emotionally," she told him. The director felt his sister had been hired to embarrass him. Despite the nepotism for which Hollywood is justly famous, and despite the closeness in the Coppola family, Francis Coppola feared that if his

sister did not perform satisfactorily, he would take the rap for nepotistic casting. (By the time he made *Godfather III,* he evidently no longer felt insecure on this point, and cast his daughter Sofia in a pivotal role.) In addition, he felt that the daughter of the Godfather should be a homely girl and

that his sister was much too attractive for the role.

There was an interesting sidelight to the casting of the splendid Robert Duvall in the role of Tom Hagen, the family *consiglieri.* Rudy Vallee wanted to play the role very badly. (That's how he probably would have played it.) The Twenties crooner

Coppola cast the exemplary character actor Robert Duvall as Tom Hagen and triggered a career.

The Great Santini (1979)

The baseball classic *The Natural* (1984)

As Dr. Watson in *The Seven-Per-Cent Solution* (1976)

The Pursuit of D.B. Cooper (1981)

Coppola cast Diane Keaton as Kay Adams though till then she had worked solely in comedy as a foil to Woody Allen.

was now in his seventies, and his name had last been in the public eye when his neighbors successfully resisted his efforts to have the city rename the street where he lived after him. When Vallee's agent communicated with Al Ruddy, the producer was stunned. "Doesn't he know," said Ruddy, "how old Tom Hagen is? He's thirty-five."

Diane Keaton distinguished herself as Kay Adams, the New England fiancée of Michael Corleone. Opinion on Diane Keaton was far from uniform. Before this she had done only comedy and was thought to be a ditzy, airhead type, a great foil for the wit of Woody Allen perhaps, but not quite the dramatic actress the role called for. There was additional concern that she would tower over "that midget Pacino." Thus, Jill Clayburgh was tested, so was Susan Blakely. Trish Van Devere was considered, along with Jennifer O'Neill, Veronica Hamel, Genevieve Bujold, Karen Black, Blythe Danner, Cybill Shepherd, and Ali MacGraw. But the role went to Diane Keaton.

Diane Keaton had played a ditzy airhead type in *Annie Hall* (1977). She was not seen as a "dramatic actress."

Reds (1981)

By seeing her potential as a dramatic actress, Coppola widened Diane Keaton's career into non-comedic films.

Mrs. Soffel (1984)

Shoot the Moon (1981)

Diane Keaton had played Mary Wilke, an aggressive intellectual, in the Woody Allen comedy *Manhattan* (1979).

Crimes of the Heart (1986)

The Little Drummer Girl (1984)

Coppola had used James Caan in his film *The Rain People*. By casting him as the hot-blooded Sonny, he propelled him into a series of high-visibility roles.

Though the role of the Gentile Kay Adams went to Diane Keaton, she probably would not have been willing to crack heads to get it. It was the Italian roles that produced such threatening impulses. Coppola had said he wanted to fill all the Italian roles with Italian actors, so when the roles of Sonny and Tom Hagen went to the non-Italian James Caan and Robert Duvall, the natives grew restless. Two mafioso types, with faces full of broken commandments, lurked across the street from the Paramount gate. Whenever a car approached, they produced signs that read "ITALIANS FOR ITALIAN ROLES" and "MORE ADVANTAGES FOR ITALIAN ACTORS." The initials of the latter sign formed an unsettling acrostic. "It's getting tough for us Italian heavies to get work," said a picketing actor with a bent nose and thick jaw.

Funny Lady (1974) with Barbra Streisand

Hide in Plain Sight (1980) with Jill Eikenberry

The Gambler (1974)

Cinderella Liberty (1973) with Marsha Mason

What further angered the Italian actors was Paramount's announcement that *The Godfather* would be cast entirely from unknowns. This brought out an army of unknowns; there are a great many of them in Hollywood, as there are in other cities. The announcement also spawned a shower of letters from people all over the country. When David Selznick declared, in search of publicity, that Scarlett O'Hara would be played by an unknown, Southern girls by the thousands waited patiently by their porticos for a visit from George Cukor. But by 1970 America's unknowns had grown more assertive. Letters rained down on Paramount's Bronson Avenue offices.

Said one letter: "I've read *The Godfather,* I'm dark haired, I weigh 235 pounds." Said another: "My father was a second generation Italian and was slightly connected with the Mafia." Said another: "I've read you may be filming in Cleveland. My father is the Godfather of Cleveland and he can make things easier for you." Said another testily: "Look, I'm flying out to Los Angeles today to try out for the film. Okay?" Wrote a proud mother: "You've got to see my three Italian sons." Another middle-aged woman sent a snapshot and said: "I'm sure when you saw my picture, your first thought was: perfect for the Don's wife. Maybe you're right, but I don't know how to make macaroni." Alas.

The flood of letters reminded one of the Hollywood joke about the determination of thespians. Two actors are in conversation:

Thief (1981) with Tom Signorelli

"What are you doing now?"

"I'm doing a one man show."·

"Is there anything in it for me?"·

Given the much publicized need for Italian actors in *The Godfather,* some actors who had changed their names to conceal their Italian ancestry, changed them back again. Others authenticated their Italian heritage by mailing in irreplaceable family albums. In a display of Latin audacity, Cubans, Mexicans, Puerto Ricans, and South Americans insisted that they were in fact

Misery (1990)

Gardens of Stone (1987)

The TV movie *Brian's Song* (1971)

Italians and solicited roles. Even some WASPs with dark complexions asserted that they were actually Italian-Americans. Price-Stern-Sloan, the west-coast publishers, reported a surge of sales on their satiric book *How To Be An Italian*.

Ethnicity is a curious thing. Abe Vigoda never claimed to be an Italian, but Coppola thought he was and gave him the meaty role of Tessio. Vigoda was Jewish. On the other hand, Alex Rocco was Italian, yet Coppola cast him to play the role of Moe Greene, the Jewish casino owner. You don't have to be Jewish to like Levy's rye and you don't have to be Jewish to play a Jew in a Coppola movie. Of

course, Rocco had another thing going for him. At his audition, he left the impression that he had spent time in prison.

Puzo's secretary, Janet Snow, was startled to receive a wire reading: MICHAEL CORLEONE ARRIVES 10 A.M. TOMORROW. The sender appeared at the Paramount gate the following morning and when he was denied admittance, followed Puzo around town for several days. Another enterprising actor actually filmed and starred in a ten-minute movie based on the novel. He played both

the roles of Michael Corleone and Tom Hagen (for Hagen he wore a mustache), doubtless on the theory that if one of the roles was already filled, he would have a shot at the other. The film had main titles, a musical score, a company of extras, and special effects.

Not only actors were drawn to the project. Melvin Belli, the famous criminal lawyer, phoned and demanded to see Mario Puzo or Al Ruddy. He sought no less than the role of Don Corleone. Evidently, hubris

Slither (1973)

thrives in the criminal courtroom.

Because Puzo had created the story, he was often sought for his support. Calls would come daily to the Puzo office, asking: "You want anyone hurt? You want any arms or legs broken?" On one occasion, three large, menacing-looking men appeared in Puzo's office. They were dressed in Forties wear, including felt hats and double-breasted suits that bulged under the armpits. "Puzo here?" one of the mugs rasped to a secretary as the other two hovered in the doorway. The girl summoned her courage and went to Puzo's assistant, Alvin Shapiro, down the hall. Shapiro produced a prop gun, took a deep breath, and flashed the weapon in front of the three huge men. They hastily took their leave.

The declining assurance of actors in the face of rejection is exemplified by one actor who sent in his resume confidently captioned: I AM MICHAEL! I AM A GOOD ACTOR! The next day, the same resumé arrived, but this time the inscription read: I THINK I'M MICHAEL AND I'M A FAIRLY GOOD ACTOR. The third day, the caption read: WELL, I THINK I JUST MIGHT DO IT.

CHAPTER 4

The Father of
The Godfather

ARGARET MITCHELL HAD written *Gone With the Wind* because she was immobilized with a broken ankle; Mario Puzo had a pile of gambling debts. Of such mundane things are blockbuster novels born.

Puzo little dreamed that in addition to making some money and paying off his bookie, he would create a movie that would bring millions to Paramount, dividends to Gulf + Western stockholders, secure the career of Francis Coppola, raise Al Pacino's price from $35,000 to over $3 million dollars a picture, revive the career of America's greatest actor, and nurture the careers of Caan, Duvall, Keaton, and Shire.

In America, the land of opportunity, *The Godfather* would also trigger numerous peripheral enterprises. For example, three talent schools, using portable videotape equipment, approached people on the street, telling them they were doing screen tests for *The Godfather*. The schools charged them one hundred dollars for tests,

with the promise that the producers would look at them. There were many takers.

No one had devoted this much attention to organized crime since Bobby Kennedy had prodded FBI director J. Edgar Hoover into making the Mafia one of its main targets. Mario Puzo aimed low and hit the stars. He wanted nothing more than to get a paperback deal on a previous novel, *The Fortunate Pilgrim,* and figured that once *The Godfather* reached the book stores, he might be able to manage it. He wrote a hundred pages of his Mafia novel and showed them to Paramount Pictures. They took an option on it for the modest sum of $12,000 and agreed to pay the novelist a total of $80,000 for movie rights and the screenplay.

Puzo had done a vast amount of research to give the book a true-to-life quality. He was able to paint a totally convincing portrait of naked power, while also implying the dire threats to a society that permitted such criminality. The novel was

eventful, dramatic, and impossible to put down. Puzo's first two novels had produced courteous critical reviews and negligible sales. They were greeted by public apathy, and the day after their publication, Puzo woke up obscure. *The Godfather* was another matter. It quickly became one of the most avidly-read books in publishing history, with a million hardcover copies and twelve million paperbacks sold before the movie appeared.

Paramount's Bob Evans knew a good thing when he saw it. Like Marc Jaffe, the prescient editor who saw an outline of Bill Blatty's *The Exorcist* and promptly made a deal to support him for a year while he wrote the novel, Evans reacted quickly. After reading the first hundred pages of the book, he installed Puzo in an office on the Paramount lot. Because Puzo wrote the novel in Paramount's offices rather than a Greenwich Village garret, thoughts of the forthcoming movie were always close at hand. He wrote some very filmable scenes.

Paramount had made another Mafia movie called *The Brotherhood* a few years before and it had bombed. But *The Godfather* posed only a modest risk. Bob Evans did not picture the movie as much more than a quickie gangster flick set in modern-day Kansas City. Yet Paramount did very well with it.

The Italian-American Civil Rights League lent a decisive hand. Just as the phrase "Banned in Boston" had helped promote many of the plays it sought to suppress, just as the Legion of Decency had aided many movies with its disapproval rating, the Italian-American League, by its indignation, drew the press's attention to the novel and the film. Puzo's book became an overnight bestseller and Paramount's film drew the kind of frenzied attention that had been produced by Selznick's spurious search for Scarlett O'Hara. *The New York Times* ran front-page stories and editorials on Paramount's seeming acquiescence to the Mafia, and Coppola was able to transform his low-budget film into a high-profile production.

Mario Puzo had done a herculean job of research and loaded his book with an array of engrossing details about Mafia crime and the Mafia clan. The book felt absolutely authentic, if a trifle flattering to the underworld. A great many critics and readers rebuked Puzo for "romanticizing the Mafia." He had, after all, portrayed the gangsters and hoods as human beings, not monsters and dragons. With disarming candor, the novelist admitted that that's just what he had done. Puzo had never met a mobster in his life. He was creating compelling novelistic narrative and provocative characterizations. Shakespeare himself had been sympathetic to quite a few villains, including Richard III. "Villains are people, aren't they?" asked Puzo.

Jack Kennedy once described himself as an idealist without any "unnecessary illusions." Puzo had few unnecessary illusions about his book. "The Mafia is certainly romanticized in *The Godfather*," he conceded. "They are much worse guys than that." Don Corleone emerged as a heroic figure of mythic dimensions. He was a marvelous father to his family and great father figure to the community. He refused to do business in narcotics or double-deal anyone. In his death scene, director Coppola has him carve monstrous teeth from an orange, as if mocking the very idea that he might be a monster. Yet the character of the Don was a synthesis of real life underworld figures Vito Genovese and Joseph Profaci. If these men dealt in drugs and sometimes betrayed an associate, Puzo's work was, after all, a novel, not a documentary.

A period on the "Gold Coast" of Hollywood was a pleasant change for Puzo. It was a welcome relief from the hermitic life of the novelist, and the payoff was more promising than just critical praise. It was the sort of atmosphere that any unappreciated novelist might enjoy. Puzo was ensconced in a Paramount office replete with an unending supply of Diet Coke in a mini-refrigerator. He had an amiable and efficient young secretary. He had a telephone with four lines and a buzzer to communicate with his secretary. He had tennis and gambling and the wonderful climate which helps make Los Angeles famous. He liked the tennis, the gambling in Las Vegas, and the propinquity of bright, bustling people on the Paramount lot.

Most people found Puzo's novel gripping and compulsively readable. For his part, Puzo may have hoped to join the company of Irving Wallace and Harold Robbins, who had written sensational bestsellers. In fact, he surpassed them. Undeniably, *The Godfather* had the juice and intensity of the Wallace-Robbins *oeuvre*. It had the slaughter and sex, the tumult and heartbreak. But it also had a greased-lightning drive. And when Puzo and Coppola transformed the book into a screenplay, it had spaciousness and vigor, with the sex and sensation somewhat diluted. The novel and its adaptation bore little relationship to the Harold Robbins' novels that had reached the screen, such as *The Carpetbaggers* and *The Adventurers*. However, like Robbins and Wallace—and like Herman Wouk and Irwin Shaw, whose books had often fueled the screen— Puzo was a superlative storyteller who provided Coppola with a wealth of incidents from which to choose.

What made the novel irresistible, in addition to Puzo's skill at the art of storytelling, was that he had taken a rich segment of American life, loaded it with sharply-defined characters and startling events, and rendered them at a pace that was swift and sure, carrying

them to an agonizing conclusion: the tragedy of a man who becomes what he doesn't want to become.

Following its publication in 1969, *The Godfather* rode the bestseller lists for no less than sixty-seven weeks. When copies began flying from the shelves and sales soared to half a million copies seemingly overnight, Coppola and Ruddy were able to convince Paramount Pictures to increase the budget and set the film in 1940's New York, despite the added expense that entailed. (This meant, among other things, dropping the reference to "hippies" in the script.)

Puzo's initial view on the final screenplay was that the director had mellowed and toned down the novel, that Coppola's characters were "too nice." Puzo said he was surprised and chagrined to learn that Hollywood screenwriters do not have as much influence as directors, producers, and studio executives. (It is a little hard to credit this kind of innocence from a man of Puzo's sophistication.) It is said that great screenplays are not written, they are rewritten, and Puzo learned the truth of this chestnut. He had done rewrite after rewrite of the script until he had had enough. Finally he

In writing the novel, Puzo had Brando in mind for Don Corleone.

told producer Ruddy that his muse had flown; his well of inspiration was dry. He could not do any more rewrites. Enough with revisions; enough with pressure; he didn't want to be involved.

At this point, Mario Puzo was effectively out of the loop. He wasn't even shown a final cut. He joked wryly about launching a Sicilian vendetta against Paramount Pictures. Puzo told of his growing distaste for the Hollywood studio system in a book called *The Godfather and Other Confessions,* released the following spring. Though it did not reach the *New York Times* bestseller list, it provided an instructive behind-the-scenes look at the making of a movie. It compares well with Lillian Ross' book on the making of *The Red Badge of Courage* and a more recent work by Julie Salamon about the filming of *Bonfire of the Vanities.*

When *The Godfather* was about to premiere in Manhattan in early 1972, Puzo was smarting. He was asked if he would attend the event. "I have a wife and five children," he snapped, "and I only have four tickets."

The novelist was clearly distressed in writing his first Hollywood screenplay. He

brings to mind the novelist, played by Dick Powell in the movie *The Bad and the Beautiful,* who is disenchanted by the movie business but learns to embrace it by the final fade-out. If Puzo found the film-making process distasteful, why did he agree to write the *Godfather* sequel? "I signed for it before I became unhappy," he said. But the novelist found he liked writing in the script form and was determined to write a perfect screenplay, a script "nobody can screw up." Puzo declared he'd like to form his own production company so he could control the development of properties. But Hollywood is tenacious in typecasting talent. Puzo had proved himself a gifted screenwriter, ergo he was hired to write the scripts for other big movies, including *Superman* (where Brando again had a role). In this movie, director Richard Donner was the guiding force. Puzo also moved on to another novel, which predictably became a bestseller.

Meanwhile, Francis Coppola had taken the screenplay that he and Puzo had fashioned, and set to work turning it into film. He delivered Puzo's book to the screen as faithfully as any reader could have wished.

David Selznick wouldn't let his screenwriters on *Gone With the Wind* use a line of dialogue that was not in Margaret Mitchell's novel. Though Coppola's fidelity fell short of this level of obsession, he remained faithful to Puzo's book. Most of the book's dramatic highlights were brought to the moviegoer, from the horse's head in the bed to the corrupt police captain in the restaurant.

The book-to-script process was an intriguing one. Coppola ripped pages from the novel and pasted them in a stage director's notebook. He described the action with notes in the margin of each page. Thus, most of the key story elements made their way onto the screen.

Coppola added depth to the relationships between Michael, Sonny, and Fredo, and gave the women in the story a more definitive part. Though women are categorically excluded from "family business," Connie was given more to do. Coppola also made explicit the ethnic minutiae and Catholic rituals. Family ceremonies like weddings, funerals, and christenings have a good deal of plot importance.

Perhaps the part of Puzo's Hollywood experience that he found most unsettling—

at his plate.

"I don't think so," said Sinatra.

The fellow wasn't very quick. He began again.

"I'd like you to meet my friend Mario Puzo," he said.

"I said I don't want to meet him," said Sinatra.

Finally the millionaire got the message. He started to cry at the thought that he had offended Sinatra.

"Frank, I'm sorry, I'm sorry. . . ."

Whereupon Sinatra began to heap abuse on Puzo. He threatened him with physical violence and called him a pimp. He suggested that if it weren't for the difference in their ages, he would beat the living daylights out of him.

"God, Frank, I didn't know. I'm so sorry. . . ."

When a friend tried to introduce Puzo to Sinatra at a restaurant, the singer lashed out at the novelist.

worse than being dropped from the loop or finding himself at the bottom of the pecking order—was his meeting with Frank Sinatra, whom he had stereotyped in his novel. When dining at Chasen's, Puzo's millionaire dinner partner noticed Sinatra sitting elsewhere in the restaurant. He dragged the reluctant novelist to Sinatra's table and insisted on introducing them.

"I'd like you to meet my good friend Mario Puzo," said the millionaire.

Sinatra continued to stare

CHAPTER 5

The Man Who Shot The Godfather

"FRANCIS BELIEVES YOU only have a chance to do something terrific if you're on the edge of disaster," said a longtime friend. If so, disaster has been a nourishing diet for Francis Ford Coppola. He expresses the inventiveness of American cinema at its best. He is the most visionary moviemaker of his era. He has introduced many exceptional actors to the screen, and got some of the screen's top actors to do their best work for him. Like Citizen Kane, Francis Coppola built and lost an empire. Yet he continues to be one of the most charismatic contenders on the film scene.

An examination of Coppola's life and work reveals the theme that made *The Godfather* so triumphantly appealing: family relationships. Family relationships have been the constant subject of Coppola's work and a continuing preoccupation in his life.

The first feature he directed, a low-budget film

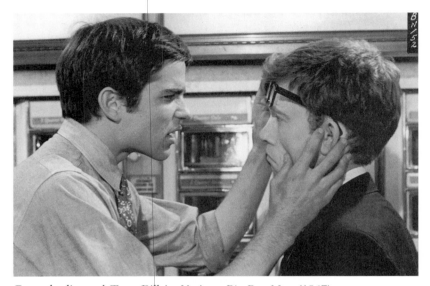

Coppola directed Tony Bill in *You're a Big Boy Now* (1967).

Coppola directed Fred Astaire in *Finian's Rainbow* (1968).

Coppola directed James Caan in *The Rain People* (1969).

called *You're a Big Boy Now,* was among a spate of youth movies of the mid–1960s. It deals with a young man trying to free himself of overbearing parents and offers a lively treatment of family relationships.

His next project for Warner Brothers, in 1968, was *Finian's Rainbow,* a job he took to impress his father. It was not a promising enterprise: a three-million-dollar budget for a film musical is small. Despite improvising all the choreography, Coppola confessed with dismay, "I know nothing about dancing." Yet he took the job. Why? His father conducted orchestras for musicals. Coppola felt his dad would be happy if his son did a musical. The director promptly phoned his father, who was conducting a road-show version of *Half a Sixpence,* and engaged him to compose music for the movie. The family comes first.

When *Finian's Rainbow* turned out disastrously, Coppola next turned to an intimate drama and directed *The Rain People* in 1969. Again its subject of family fascinated Coppola. The movie focuses on the hero's intense commitment to family. However, audiences did not show commitment to the film.

In 1969, Coppola extracted a loan from Warner Brothers and he and George Lucas formed a film company in San Francisco. They called the new company American Zoetrope. They wanted to create an alternative to the Hollywood establishment, a utopia where they could form a "family of talents" to give creative people a chance to make movies that otherwise wouldn't be made. But in Hollywood, Utopia is not a holy grail, except in occasional movies like *Lost Horizon.*

When Zoetrope's first film, George Lucas' *THX-1138,* made in 1971, did not become a box office success, Warner Brothers cancelled its support of the fledgling company. Warners also demanded that Coppola repay the loan. But when God closes a door He opens a window. Warner's call for reimbursement pressed Coppola to agree to direct *The Godfather.* It was a decision not without precedent. Clark Gable agreed to play Rhett Butler because of money when MGM agreed to pay off his first wife, freeing him to marry Carole Lombard.

But when Coppola got around to reading Mario Puzo's novel, he didn't like it much. After all, Coppola wanted to do small films, personal films, art films, films

about family. Of course, it could be said that this was a film about family. . . .

On the day he first met with the Paramount brass, he called his father to say: "They want me to direct this hunk of trash." His father had not read the book but told his talented son to make the film anyway, "Make some money, Francis, then you can do what you want."

The film had the side effect of bringing Carmine Coppola to Hollywood to stay. He contributed to the score of *The Godfather,* adding incidental music to the main theme and providing most of the music for the wedding scene that launched the film and established its mood.

Francis' father was not the only member of the family whose career was advanced by *The Godfather.* The director's sister Talia, married to composer David Shire at the time, had her own creative interests. Her psychiatrist urged her to ask her brother for a role in the film, sensing that Talia wanted to become more assertive in the family circle. Daughters in high-achievement families, especially Italian ones, often find their intellectual gifts and creative talents eclipsed

when parental attention turns to the sons. So it was with Talia, growing up in the shadow of the brilliant Francis. Yet while Francis said no to a role for Talia, Bob Evans auditioned her and selected her for the role of Connie.

The Godfather was besieged by trouble from first to last. It was assaulted by an Italian-American lobby for its seeming slur on the Italian community. Furthermore, even the studio viewed it doubtfully because of its casting: Marlon Brando, Al Pacino, James Caan and Robert Duvall. Shortly before its premiere, the movie industry was awash with gossip that the film was a calamity. Some calamity! Negative predictions notwithstanding, *The Godfather* opened to an avalanche of applause from critics and public. The Mafia "family" he had brought to the screen rewarded Coppola handsomely.

Exhilarated by his triumph, Francis Coppola submerged himself in work. He had brought Puzo to the screen; now he adapted F. Scott Fitzgerald's *The Great Gatsby.* He was setting out to disprove Fitzgerald's famous line, "There are no second acts in American lives." He

Coppola wrote the screenplay of *The Great Gatsby* (1974).

Coppola produced and George Lucas directed *American Graffiti* (1985).

launched a weekly magazine in San Francisco called *City*. He produced *American Graffiti* for George Lucas, which proved another resounding financial and critical success. Coppola wrote and directed a Kafkaesque horror story called *The Conversation*. With this film, he was anxious to demonstrate that he was not dependent on a book for his best work. Coppola wanted to show he could create an original script of value, and he succeeded.

When Coppola co-wrote the screenplay of *The Godfather, Part II* with Mario Puzo, and then directed the movie, his motives were somewhat different. Coppola wanted to demolish the idyllic image he had spun around the Mafia family. By painting a picture of an idealized, romanticized mafioso clan in that first film, he had done his job not wisely but too well. In *Part II* he brutally undercut the image of family love he had celebrated by picturing its decline and decay. The vision of filial devotion curdles. Michael's wife leaves him after aborting their unborn child; Michael orders the murder of his brother Fredo. There is a general coarsening of behavior. "This time I really set out to destroy the family," said the director. Again he succeeded.

Coppola had accumulated an extraordinary roster of achievement, including a string of personal Oscars. This was the only example of both a movie and its sequel winning Best Movie Academy Awards. Successful, Coppola now reached for a fresh challenge. He is a man who, as one observer put it, "bites off more than he can chew and then chews it." He wanted new excitement and found it in the creation of *Apocalypse Now*. The film documentary, *Hearts of Darkness,* that his wife Eleanor crafted, about the making of the film, expresses the dimensions of this new adventure.

During this period, Coppola enjoyed indulgences that burdened his marriage.

Coppola directed Gene Hackman in *The Conversation* (1974).

His wife Eleanor was an accomplished artist who had submerged her own artistic impulses in favor of caring for Francis and the kids. *Apocalypse Now* placed an undue strain on Francis' family. Said his sister, Talia, "Nobody really understood what happened when movies were taken off the back lot. In those days a man could come back home to his family at the end of the day. . . . When you go out on location it's different. Francis was two years on *Apocalypse*. He brought his family out there to get lice in their hair. It cost him spiritually."

Talia spoke frankly of the hazards that came with her brother's new celebrity. "A person starts to get famous and the very thing that he needs to remain extraordinary starts to fall away." Instead of candor and friendship, he gets "an entourage who will tell you whatever you want to hear. . . . All of a sudden your only friends are your bodyguards."

Coppola created something exceptional in the Philippines, and when he got back to Hollywood, he sat back and watched Robert Benton's *Kramer vs. Kramer* grab all the Oscars. Ironically, it was a story about family. By this time, the San Francisco-based

Zoetrope was no more. But in 1979 Coppola bought the old Hollywood General Studios and made it a new refuge for talented moviemakers who were not members of the Hollywood establishment. But things turned sour again. A project called *Hammett* engaged Coppola's attention. When it was virtually completed, he stopped production and ordered the script rewritten. The movie did little business. Somewhere the great writer Dashiell Hammett was moaning.

Coppola's own *One From the Heart* followed. Planned as an intimate, personal film, its budget ballooned and it proved an artistic and financial disappointment.

Like Alfred Hitchcock and John Huston, Francis Ford Coppola is as fascinating as his best movies. And his best movies have been exceedingly good. Those who despair at his failures should remember that Hitchcock made his *Topaz* and John Huston his *The Barbarian and the Geisha*. Coppola's work includes several masterpieces of extraordinary power that have been both immensely profitable and popular.

It is fascinating to follow Coppola's career—which has many fertile years ahead. He

is interesting as an artist, as a patron, as a visionary, and as the embodiment of a singular success story. Just as Don Corleone is the larger-than-life hero of the *Godfather* saga, Francis Ford Coppola is the larger-than-life hero of his own special Hollywood saga.

(PREVIOUS PAGES)
Coppola directed the antiwar epic *Apocalypse Now* (1979).

Coppola was disappointed when *Apocalypse Now* lost the Best Picture Oscar to Robert Benton's *Kramer Vs Kramer*.

Coppola directed his romantic *One from the Heart* (1982).

Coppola won an Oscar for his screenplay for *Patton* (1970).

Coppola directed Matt Dillon and Mickey Rourke in *Rumble Fish* (1983).

Coppola directed Kathleen Turner in *Peggy Sue Got Married* (1986).

Coppola directed Richard Gere in *The Cotton Club* (1984).

Coppola directed Jeff Bridges in *Tucker* (1988).

CHAPTER 6

The Selling of The Godfather

A RISING TIDE LIFTS ALL boats, and *The Godfather* benefited all movies of its time. The box office success of the Coppola film was of such extraordinary dimensions, that it served as a siren song to call moviegoers back to the movie theaters they had been ignoring. The huge proportions of this historic smash were such that it seemed to raise the movie business Lazarus-like from the dead, or at least, the doldrums.

Moviemakers often lean to hyperbole—whether discussing success or failure— but it was certainly true that in 1972 the movies were perceived by some as an expiring business. But *The Godfather,* and the savvy marketing on which it rode to unprecedented heights, seemed to be single-handedly reviving the ardor of the moviegoing public. A nervous industry was having a renaissance. The movie business had found a fresh reason for optimism.

Hollywood was as ecstatic as if they had found a new sex goddess. For awhile it seemed impossible to get the public to desert its television set, hire a babysitter, park the car, buy the tickets and popcorn, and settle back for a couple of hours in the dark. Faced with this defection in the Fifties, Hollywood had used Cinemascope and 3-D. In the Seventies, it used *The Godfather* to remind America that movies were better than ever.

In the teeth of the industry's solemn talk, *The Godfather* provided a surefire rule for success. The formula seemed to be (1) take a best-selling novel, (2) add a screenplay with a strong narrative drive, (3) mix in a formidable director, (4) add inspired casting, (5) publicize the film boldly before it goes in front of the camera, and (6) launch an audacious plan of promotion when it's ready for release.

The studio publicity machinery did a superb job. They landed the movie on the front covers of America's three leading weekly newsmagazines. (Lee Iacocca only made two of them when he introduced the Mustang.) The publicity department also placed prominent articles in a large number of leading magazines and newspapers. And through effective salesmanship, Paramount gained the cooperation of theater owners, who spurred popular reaction that fed a big response at the box office.

The Godfather gave new meaning to that most joyous of Hollywood words, "blockbuster." Frank Yablans, who had replaced Stanley Jaffe as Paramount's president by the time of *The Godfather*'s release, was the right man in the right place at the right time. Yablans had been the studio's sales chief and his superior marketing skills were thrown into high gear. He mounted a Midas-sized advertising budget for the film, he raised ticket prices, and he opened the movie boldly in thousands of theaters. In later years, this strategy became more commonplace, but in 1972 it was revolutionary.

PARAMOUNT PICTURES PRESENTS

The Godfather

AN
Albert S. Ruddy
PRODUCTION

STARRING

Marlon Brando

AND

Al Pacino   James Caan   Richard Castellano   Robert Duvall
Sterling Hayden   John Marley   Richard Conte   Diane Keaton

PRODUCED BY   DIRECTED BY   SCREENPLAY BY
Albert S. Ruddy   Francis Ford Coppola   Mario Puzo AND Francis Ford Coppola
BASED ON
Mario Puzo's NOVEL "The Godfather"   MUSIC
                                      SCORED BY Nino Rota   Color By Technicolor® A Paramount Picture

R RESTRICTED
Under 17 requires accompanying
Parent or Adult Guardian   SOUNDTRACK ALBUM AVAILABLE ON PARAMOUNT RECORDS

The Godfather opened to incredibly long lines. The poor are always with us, and they were very much in evidence in the long lines in midtown Manhattan. The vagrants of 42nd Street quickly discerned that they could take their place in line, and when they were close to the box office, hawk their place for twenty dollars to more affluent members of the community.

Elsewhere in town, other Marlon Brando films were popping up on movie marquees. Before *The Godfather,* at least a dozen Brando films had caused people to stay away in droves, but now anything bearing his name was a magnet, from the memorable *Viva Zapata* to the forgettable *Burn!* The denizens of Wall Street also profited as the price for a share of Gulf + Western stock vaulted from thirty-eight dollars to forty-four dollars. Newspapers ran editorials, op-ed pieces, stories and features, and the Entertainment sections boasted articles, interviews, and reviews.

Public memory is short, and by now many people have forgotten the frenzy to see *The Godfather* that engulfed America at its debut. It was like the hunger

to see *My Fair Lady* when tickets were scarce and "hot". Moviegoers employed all manner of tricks and pretexts to get to the front of the line. The stratagems were numerous. One theater owner reported, "I had people tell me they were about to faint, then when I got them inside, they recovered in a hurry." Said another exhibitor, "Some women insisted they were pregnant and couldn't stand for long periods." In one weekend a security guard was offered hundreds of dollars in bribes to allow quicker admittance, and a wide-eyed usher was offered one hundred dollars by an eager patron. One couple who stood in line for hours happily announced that they were going to *The Godfather* to celebrate their divorce.

The Godfather seemed to be playing at all hours of the day and night. Some theaters showed the film as early as 9:00 A.M. and as late as midnight. Movie screens were bright eighteen hours a day with images of the Corleone family. In cities where the film showed in several theaters, exhibitors added to public convenience by scheduling staggered playing times. Five New York theaters varied the starting time so people could

see the film without undue disruption of their working hours, dinner hours, or school hours.

Since most theaters were squeezing in six or seven showings of the three-hour film each day, they scarcely had time to empty and fill the auditoriums and sweep up the scattered popcorn. Some frantic moviegoers found, to their dismay, that there was a mere five minutes between shows. And when a theater scheduled a late-late show, a patron might leave the film, with its explicit violence, and find himself on an empty street at 6:00 A.M., where he might encounter crime firsthand.

The O'Hara Family and the Von Trapp Family were easily passed by the Corleone Family. Until *The Godfather* came along, the top-grossing films in Hollywood history had been *Gone With the Wind* (seventy-three million dollars) and *The Sound of Music* (sixty-four million dollars). Coppola's film overtook *Gone With the Wind* in a mere six months.

The axiom that "Nothing succeeds like success" was proven in the foreign markets. Paramount set out to attack the international scene with four more versions of *The Godfather*—in French, German, Italian, and

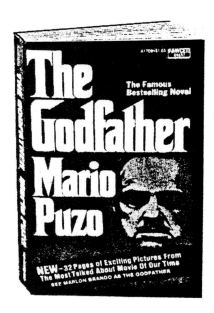

The bestselling novel by Mario Puzo

The bestselling album of the musical score

Spanish—and they hired the best writers, actors, and directors to create them. The translations, dubbing, and editing would need to be examplars of the art of adapting sound tracks. The creation of these foreign editions was supervised personally by Bob Evans, who wanted to make each one as successful in its target country as the original was in the U.S. As soon as Evans laid the groundwork for these new *Godfathers,* he announced that he would return to Hollywood to sink his teeth into the inevitable sequel to his blockbuster. It was titled tentatively *Don Michael.*

Curiously, the one place where the movie didn't fare too well was on U.S. military bases overseas. While the foreign versions of the film were packing them in in every capital in Europe, half the seats were empty in movie houses on American military bases. This suggests that violence holds little appeal for men whose intrinsic business is violence in war. But, realistically, the explanation is simpler: The price of tickets had been set above the norm for army bases. A pricey $1.50 for adults and 75 cents for children more than doubled the usual cost of 75 cents for adults and 25 cents for kids.

The Godfather also spawned a vast array of products including a *Godfather* board game, Mafia-style fedoras and, of course, *The Godfather* soundtrack album. There was also Godfather spaghetti, Godfather pizza franchises, Godfather hero shops, and Godfather lemon-ice stands. The film also encouraged some comic record albums: *Everything You Always Wanted to Know About the Godfather But Don't Ask,* and a takeoff titled *The Firsta Family.*

Millions of copies of the novel were already in print, and with the success of the film, Fawcett Publications put one-and-a-half million more paperbacks on the racks. That brought the total number of copies in print to ten million. For a while at least, *The Godfather* showed signs of outselling *The Bible,* whose injunctions the Corleones tended to ignore. But that wasn't the end of it. A paperback called *The Godmother* was also published, and a formerly-made French film was renamed *The Godson.*

Another well-read book of the period was Paramount's Press Book, a document laden with exploitation tips for theater owners. One of these was "The Marlon Brando Radio Contest." Paramount's promotion executives suggested that exhibitors take advantage of Brando's career by creating a radio promotion focused on his past films: "Have one of your local deejays read a question relating to one of Brando's films, and the first listener to call in with the correct answer will win two tickets to your theater for the opening of *The Godfather.*" A sample of these questions was provided:

1. Brando won acclaim for his portrayal of Mark Antony in the 1953 film version of which Shakespeare classic?
2. A well-deserved Academy Award was given to Brando for which film about life on the New York docks?
3. Brando sang songs such as "Luck Be a Lady" and "I'll Know" in which 1955 musical?
4. Brando proved his talents behind the camera when he directed which Western about revenge?
5. Co-starring with Sophia Loren, Brando proved his comedy talent in which 1966 film directed by Charlie Chaplin?

The questions were not very demanding, aimed at encouraging maximum response.

(Answers:
1. *Julius Caesar*
2. *On the Waterfront*
3. *Guys and Dolls*
4. *One Eyed Jacks*
5. *A Countess from Hong Kong*)

If Coppola had agreed to make *The Godfather* a contemporary film rather than setting it in the same period as Puzo's novel, he would have shut the door on one effective form of promotion. With the movie, there dawned a new era of Forties fashions. Local department stores were offering long dresses and platform shoes for the women and broad-brimmed hats, wide neckties, wide-lapelled suits, and bulky overcoats for the men. Theater owners were urged to make obvious tie-ins with local stores to produce publicity that would be useful to them both. It was recommended that exhibitors contact their city's largest department store and suggest they use the *Godfather* theme to focus attention on the store's circa-Forties fashions. The store could decorate their windows with fashions in the *Godfather* mode, encircle them with display cards, photos, and posters for the film, and then support the promotion with newspaper ads.

The Godfather brought success to entrepreneurs in a wide variety of fields, from games to pizza, from books to fedoras. That is, after all, the American way—the spirit of aggressive capitalism that was (at least by analogy) glorified in the film.

A Gallery from the Original *Godfather*

The Godfather

PARAMOUNT PICTURES PRESENTS

AN
Albert S. Ruddy
PRODUCTION

STARRING Marlon Brando
AND

The Godfather

Al Pacino   James Caan   Richard Castellano   Robert Duvall
Sterling Hayden   John Marley   Richard Conte   Diane Keaton

PRODUCED BY   DIRECTED BY   SCREENPLAY BY
Albert S. Ruddy   Francis Ford Coppola   Mario Puzo AND Francis Ford Coppola
BASED ON
Mario Puzo NOVEL   The Godfather   MUSIC SCORED BY Nino Rota   Color By Technicolor   A Paramount
Picture

SOUNDTRACK ALBUM AVAILABLE ON PARAMOUNT RECORDS

R

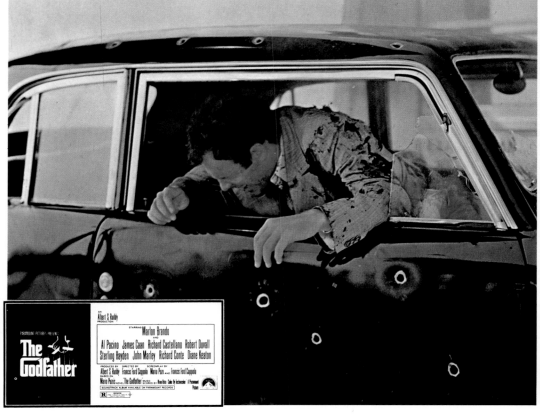

PARAMOUNT PICTURES PRESENTS

AN
Albert S. Ruddy
PRODUCTION

STARRING Marlon Brando
AND

The Godfather

Al Pacino   James Caan   Richard Castellano   Robert Duvall
Sterling Hayden   John Marley   Richard Conte   Diane Keaton

PRODUCED BY   DIRECTED BY   SCREENPLAY BY
Albert S. Ruddy   Francis Ford Coppola   Mario Puzo AND Francis Ford Coppola
BASED ON
Mario Puzo NOVEL   The Godfather   MUSIC SCORED BY Nino Rota   Color By Technicolor   A Paramount
Picture

SOUNDTRACK ALBUM AVAILABLE ON PARAMOUNT RECORDS

R

PARAMOUNT PICTURES PRESENTS

AN
Albert S. Ruddy
PRODUCTION

STARRING **Marlon Brando**
AND

Al Pacino   James Caan   Richard Castellano   Robert Duvall
Sterling Hayden   John Marley   Richard Conte   Diane Keaton

The Godfather

PRODUCED BY   DIRECTED BY   SCREENPLAY BY
Albert S. Ruddy   Francis Ford Coppola   Mario Puzo AND Francis Ford Coppola
BASED ON
Mario Puzo's NOVEL "The Godfather"   MUSIC SCORED BY Nino Rota   Color By Technicolor   A Paramount
Picture
R   SOUNDTRACK ALBUM AVAILABLE ON PARAMOUNT RECORDS

PARAMOUNT PICTURES PRESENTS

The Godfather

AN
Albert S. Ruddy
PRODUCTION

STARRING
Marlon Brando
AND
Al Pacino · James Caan · Richard Castellano · Robert Duvall
Sterling Hayden · John Marley · Richard Conte · Diane Keaton

PRODUCED BY   DIRECTED BY   SCREENPLAY BY
Albert S. Ruddy   Francis Ford Coppola   Mario Puzo and Francis Ford Coppola
BASED ON
Mario Puzo's NOVEL "The Godfather" MUSIC SCORED BY Nino Rota · Color By Technicolor® A Paramount
Picture
SOUNDTRACK ALBUM AVAILABLE ON PARAMOUNT RECORDS

R

CHAPTER 7

Barzini to Jones

Censors often help the things they try to suppress, bringing publicity to the things they deplore. When the Italian-American League tried to sanitize *The Godfather,* they did not plan to feed the flames of notoriety and help make the film a gigantic success.

In early 1971, when Mario Puzo was still laboring on the screenplay, producer Al Ruddy was not all that convinced of the beneficial side effects of censorship. With good reason, Ruddy feared that given the opposition of the powerful Italian-American League, *The Godfather* might never be made. Italians, it seemed, were livid over the likelihood that the movie would imply that to be Italian was to be a mobster. Ruddy was a cool, shrewd, forceful fellow, yet after receiving twenty menacing phone calls at his Paramount office, he would have been reckless not to be concerned. He acquired a .45-caliber automatic and kept it in his desk along with the paper clips and the script revisions. When he chanced to switch cars with his secretary, she reported the

next morning that she found the vehicle riddled with bullet holes.

The League's war chest needed replenishing to fight *The Godfather,* so Frank Sinatra held a mammoth rally in Madison Square Garden for the apparent purpose of stopping the filming. Given the popularity of the singer and the strong emotions involved, the affair raised $600,000. When contacted by location staffers, many Italian-American shopkeepers in New York City were uncooperative about letting Coppola shoot on their premises. About a hundred letters arrived at the Paramount mailroom from U.S. Congressmen and Senators. One presidential candidate had written. It was unwise to underestimate the power of the Italian-American community.

There was no question that the Italian-American League had teeth. Shortly before, the League had picketed the *Staten Island Advance,* a newspaper that used the noun "Mafia" in its articles dealing with alleged members of Mafia families residing on Staten Island.

Frank Sinatra held a mammoth rally at Madison Square Garden and raised $600,000 to fill the war chest of the Italian American League, which was trying to suppress *The Godfather.*

The protest went beyond picketing and letter-writing. A newspaper delivery truck was burned and two delivery men were brutalized. Specifically, they were forced to lie face down in the back of their truck, while mobsters set their papers afire, closed the rear door on the truck and told them they would be shot if they emerged.

These threats to public tranquility were causing dread and trepidation at the offices of Gulf + Western, Paramount's parent company. The powers ordered Al Ruddy to deal with the problem. (So you want to be a movie producer, do you?) Ruddy set out to make peace, if possible, with the Italian-American community. He met with representatives of the League at the Park Sheraton Hotel.

Ruddy made it clear to them that it was not his intention to defame any ethnic group. He actually turned over a copy of the screenplay to Joe Colombo, head of the League. The Italian-American League wanted all reference to the Mafia or the Cosa Nostra deleted from the script. They wanted Ruddy to drop the Italian-sounding names and use "names like Smith and Jones and Johnson" for the gangsters. Ruddy bridled. He agreed to drop the words "Mafia" and "Cosa Nostra" —they only appeared twice in the entire script and were unnecessary to convey Coppola's vision. The phrase "Five Families" would serve as well. As James Caan said wryly, "Nobody's gonna think it's a picture about the Irish Republican Army." Ruddy also agreed to people the gang with some actors

John Mitchell, Richard Nixon's attorney general, banned the words "Mafia" and "Cosa Nostra" from the speeches and releases of the FBI, as offensive to Italian Americans.

who were not of Italian extraction.

Ruddy even vowed to turn over the proceeds from the movie's premiere to the League for its hospital fund. Now it was Paramount's turn to bridle. They had not objected to the loss of a couple of proper nouns. After all, Richard Nixon's Attorney General, John Mitchell, had banned the words from speeches and releases of the FBI as offensive to Italian-Americans. New York Governor Nelson Rockefeller had ordered state police to cleanse their vocabulary of the words. The *New York Post* regularly substituted the word "mob" or "underworld" for "Mafia" after receiving protesting letters from Italian readers.

But the business of turning over the proceeds of the movie's premiere caused corporate chagrin. Nobody had authorized that. *Variety,* the show business daily, headlined, "PAR BURNS OVER GODFATHER DEAL BUT WILL RUB OUT MAFIA."

Paramount was also taking offense at the notoriety Ruddy's negotiations were producing. After all, it looked to the public and the press like the producer and his studio had knuckled under and would mutilate the film to appease its detractors. *The New York Times* took Ruddy to task in an editorial. (You can't buy that kind of publicity.) It said that the purpose of the League was to influence public opinion and congressional policy. It deplored Ruddy's craven bargain.

But Francis Coppola was unconcerned. He knew that the deletion of a word or two would not change the basic tone of his movie, and indeed it did not. It was clear what the film was about. Said Coppola, "In the way I'd chosen to make the film, it was unnecessary to say Mafia. They *are* Mafia." At one point the director told reporters that he didn't actually feel bound by Ruddy's agreement, which must have caused the

Most Mafia members liked the film and the glorified image presented by Brando-Pacino-Caan. One critic said that rather than suppress the film, the League should have subsidized it.

producer some distress. In fact, Coppola declared there was one scene where he would like to use the word "Mafia" after all. (He never did.)

Some members of the mob lingered around the set, and proved helpful to the production. James Caan, who played the pivotal role of Sonny, strengthened his performance by watching and chatting with members of the mob. "I noticed," he said, "how they're always touching themselves. Thumbs in the belt, touching the jaw, adjusting the shirt, gripping the crotch, shirt open, tie loose. . . ."

As shooting began, Paramount President Stanley Jaffe resigned and was replaced by Frank Yablans, Paramount's former sales chief. Rumors on the set suggested that Jaffe had been the architect of his own downfall. He had wanted Ruddy dismissed for the way he managed the League affair, but the board of directors had gone against him.

On the advice of Mario Puzo, Coppola distanced himself from the mob. Though Puzo had never met a real gangster, he had researched their ways and whims carefully. Said the director, "Puzo told me . . .

Joe Valachi, a Mafia member, testified to the workings of the Mafia before a committee of the U.S. Senate and was the subject of a bestseller by Peter Maas, *The Valachi Papers*.

Mafia guys love the glamour of show business and that if you let them they'd get involved. So Mario told me I'd probably be contacted, and when I was, I should refuse to open up to them. . . . Because they respect that attitude. If you turn them off, they won't intrude into your life."

Not surprisingly, the Mafia adored the film. Coppola was accused of glorifying the underworld with his movie, just as Puzo had done with his novel. This indictment was so common that in the sequel Coppola set out to tarnish the glory and glamour by taking the Corleone family down the road to decay.

There is a delicious paradox in the Mafia as seen through the eyes of Puzo,

Coppola, and others who have written knowingly about the Mafia, such as Gay Talese in *Honor Thy Father*, Jimmy Breslin in *The Gang That Couldn't Shoot Straight*, and Peter Maas in *The Valachi Papers*. Mafia men present an image of flashy, lavish brigands, bold bandits at their most colorful. Yet these same men—"good fellas" they are called—display in their private lives the most self-righteous code of behavior. Mafia youngsters, as described by Talese or Breslin or Puzo, behave impeccably, showing a respect to their parents that has grown obsolete in more law-abiding circles. And Mafia parents are patriotic to a fault. They are foursquare spokesmen for capitalism and the entrepreneurial spirit.

CHAPTER 8

The Criticism

THE WALL STREET JOURNAL.

Los Angeles Times

THE NEW REPUBLIC

Newsweek

Esquire

New York

*L*EXICON OF MUSICAL *L*INVECTIVE by Nicholas Slonimsky is an uproarious little book. It is an anthology of criticism of various timeless musical works. It is amazing to read the scorn and ridicule that was heaped on certain great works. Said a critic of Beethoven's Ninth, "The symphony is precisely one hour and five minutes long, a fearful period indeed, which puts the patience of the audience to a severe trial." Said another caustic reviewer, "Tchaikovsky's First Piano Concerto, like the first pancake, is a flop."

Criticism has been similarly heaped on some great movies, from *Citizen Kane* to *Seven Samurai* to *The Godfather*. The latter enjoyed almost uniform praise from all quarters of the critical community. But it is intriguing (and somewhat appalling) to read the rare outbursts of opprobrium addressed to *The Godfather* and its much praised sequel. (The second sequel ran into rougher sledding.)

Much of the criticism of the original *Godfather* centered on the fact that it seemed to glorify and sanitize the Mafia, suggesting the Corleone family was peopled by compassionate, admirable, and heroic members.

Marlon Brando's performance received a tornado of praise, but there was an occasional catcall that seemed, on the whole, unjustified. Stanley Kauffman quibbled in the *New Republic*:

THE NEW REPUBLIC

Hurricane Marlon is sweeping the country, and I wish it were more than hot air. [Critics say that] the lapsed Great Actor has regained himself. . . . But from the opening line, with his back toward us, Brando reveals that he hasn't even got the man's force under control. . . . I didn't see how any gifted actor could have done less than Brando does here.

Arthur Schlesinger, Jr., historian and sometime film critic, found the movie cast a spell far beyond its merits. He said that this was the sort of gangster film that Warner Brothers would have made in the Forties as a ninety-minute feature, lively and economical. Groused Schlesinger:

In the hands of Francis Coppola, it has swelled into an overblown, pretentious, slow, and ultimately tedious three-hour quasi-epic. Gangsters at last have their Greatest Story Ever Told. . . . My guess is that three years from now . . . The Godfather will become a vague memory.

Schlesinger is a historian and perhaps he should stick to the past; he is not as good at predicting the future. Twenty years after the release of *The Godfather*, it is well remembered and constantly viewed on television and cassettes. (On the right, William F. Buckley, writing in *The New York Post*, was as poor a prophet as Schlesinger. Buckley said, "Far from surviving . . . as the *Gone With the Wind* of gangster movies, my guess is that *The Godfather* will be as quickly forgotten as it deserves to be.")

Arthur Schlesinger was also concerned that the Mafia was not presented in a villainous light.

The Mafia . . . comes over as a group of amiable businessmen, a little rough in their methods, true . . . but still loyal to that crusty old do-gooder, the Godfather. . . . Why the Italian American Civil Rights League should have raised such a fuss about the movie is a puzzle; these defenders of Italian virtue should have subsidized it.

Some London critics censured *The Godfather*. They were disturbed by the film's violent theme. Said Donald Zec in the *Daily Mirror*:

It is vicious, it is brutal, and I doubt whether such casual and unremitting slaughter has ever before been matched in a single motion picture. . . . What you see is a piece of gangster entertainment that glosses over and glamourizes a pretty squalid era of American history. No amount of sugar can sweeten that particular dill.

Edward Sorel in *Esquire* also deplored the fact that Coppola had set the audiences to rooting for felons. He said:

Esquire

Mafia boss Vito Corleone was depicted as a sort of Sicilian Robin Hood who committed violence only in retaliation or on behalf of the downtrodden. Sonny, a feared hit man in Mario Puzo's novel, became in the film merely a hothead with an overactive sex drive. . . . [There was] hardly a word about loan-sharking, prostitution, or anything else that might have kept audiences from empathizing with the band of antisocial activists.

Judith Crist also found the whitewashing of the Mafia intolerable. She wrote in *New York* magazine:

NEW YORK

The Godfather is as good as the novel—and essentially as immoral and

therefore . . . far more dangerous. . . . The whole function of this film is to show us that Hitler is a grand sort of family man, gentle with children. . . .

The Godfather, Part II, like the original, took some occasional hits. In reviewing the sequel, John Simon, famous for the eloquent and unremitting flood of vitriol in which he has doused many popular plays and films, had this to say:

What makes The Godfather, Part II *slightly more attractive than* Part I *is . . . the absence of Marlon Brando. For Brando gave an unpardonably cheap performance . . . the kind that consists entirely of some phony accent, a fixedly vacant stare, and eternities of portentous pauses. . . . The Godfather seemed to me one of the sleazier films to achieve overwhelming public and considerable critical success. Yet there is logic in this.*

For this all-time top-grossing picture is followed by The Sound of Music. *. . . And these two films are two sides of one soiled and worn-smooth coin: family pictures in the same sickening sense. . . . There was nothing to think about in* The Godfather *except when, of what sort, and how big the next bloodletting will be.*

Vincent Canby wrote in the *New York Times* that it was not as good as its predecessor:

The New York Times

The only remarkable thing about . . . Part II *is the insistent manner in which it recalls how much better the original film was. . . . It's a Frankenstein monster stitched together from leftover parts. It talks. It moves in fits and starts, but it has no mind of its own. A thick fog of boredom . . . settles in before the film is even one hour old. Part II is as stuffed with material as a Christmas goose. It's a mass (sometimes mess) of plots, subplots, characters, alliances, betrayals, ambushes, renunciations, kisses of death, you name it. Much of the time it's next to impossible to figure out who's doing what to whom. . . .*

The *Wall Street Journal* ran an editorial that denounced not the film, but its pessimistic tone, and labelled it one of a deplorable genre:

THE WALL STREET JOURNAL

A new group of movies is now putting in an appearance at your local theaters. These are what might be called 'life is not worth living movies.' The most prominent among them is The Godfather, Part II. . . . *However much [the original* Godfather *movie] glorified criminals, it also glorified hard work and ambition and toughness. . . . Not so* The Godfather, Part II. . . . *The society in*

The Godfather, Part II is thoroughly sick and ugly, as is everyone in it. Corruption, brutality and violence are the only constants. No one can be trusted and no one emerges as admirable. . . . It is depressing to see an art form take such a dim view of the human condition.

Paul Zimmerman in *Newsweek,* who had praised the original, was less sanguine about its sequel. He said:

Newsweek

We grow restless watching the predictable played out at a crawl and impatient for some liberating energy of sudden surprise. . . . This extended, highly personal coda makes one hungry for the relatively uncomplicated entertainment values of the original. If Godfather II *is less satisfying than its predecessor, it is because it refuses to answer this*

perhaps vulgar but nonetheless real need. Somehow this . . . film never pulls us once and for all into its own world.

Playgirl magazine, renowned for presenting a centerfold of Burt Reynolds in the buff, referred to the movie as the story of "what happens when a college boy takes over the Mafia" and announced dismissively:

PLAYGIRL

Unfortunately the movie never gets off the ground, and the story is bogged down in a series of isolated scenes. . . . The overall effect is one of incoherence and sluggishness. The seams show, the momentum is repeatedly lost; and in a movie this long, one becomes frustrated and, finally, bored.

John Simon had praised *Part II* for the absence of Brando, but Molly Haskell had the good sense to complain about his absence. She wrote in the *Village Voice* under the headline "CORLEONE SAGA SAGS":

the village VOICE

Brando's absence hangs over the new picture as his presence hung over the previous one. . . . The characters are not only not mythic—they are not even very interesting. The actual dialogue could be contained on the back of a grocery list.

Critic Joy Gould Boyum, writing in the *Wall Street Journal,* which had dismissed the film editorially for its grim view of the human condition, also missed Brando. She wrote:

THE WALL STREET JOURNAL

What made The Godfather *work as well as it did was the Godfather himself. . . . That hoary villain-hero is missing from* The Godfather, Part II

and it is largely his absence that explains the film's failure. [Coppola and Puzo] have tried to do it this time without a central figure of epic dimensions whose magnified personality can sustain our interest and bring together the film's diverse episodes. . . . They have essentially tried to give us an 'El Cid' without the Cid.

Godfather Part III, so long in coming, commanded as much media attention as an outbreak of war. But though magazines and newspapers trumpeted the coming, when it arrived, they were less ecstatic than they had been with *Parts I* and *II*. Coppola had spoiled the critics with two masterpieces. Now they would settle for nothing less. Some critics faulted the casting of Sofia Coppola, the director's teenage daughter, in a pivotal role.

Said *Time*'s Richard Corliss, "Her gosling gracelessness comes close to wrecking the movie."

The *New York Post*'s Jami Bernard went further, declaring, "Coppola has

virtually ruined his movie by casting her," and added gratuitously, "there'll be hell to pay around the Coppola house after Sofia's notices come out."

Gene Siskel of "Siskel & Ebert at the Movies" found her "out of her acting league."

The *Boston Phoenix*'s Peter Keough, with a smirk at the director's financial woes and recent film failures, observed that while Michael Corleone was in need of redemption, "Coppola is even more so— not just from debts but from mediocrity."

Few critics compared *Part III* favorably to its predecessors. Some added insult to injury by bluntly dismissing it as a major failure.

The *Charlotte Observer*'s Lawrence Toppman referred to "ludicrous plot twists" and "shallow characterizations," adding "the central plot crowds in subplots and extraneous details like a mammoth sinking into a tar pit."

The *Los Angeles Times*' Michael Wilmington expressed disappointment with the script and said the film was inevitably flawed by the loss of Robert Duvall's Tom Hagen character.

If Coppola felt distressed by any of the criticism, he might recall the words that were directed at another prodigious work by an American back in the Twenties. The review is forgotten but the work is well remembered. Said a critic of George Gershwin's *Rhapsody in Blue:*

How trite and feeble and conventional the tunes are. How sentimental and vapid the harmonic treatment, under its disguise of fussy and futile counterpoint. . . . Weep over the lifelessness of the melody and harmony, so derivative, so stale, so inexpressive.

Coppola is in good company. Gershwin, Beethoven and Tchaikovsky have all been savaged by unremembered critics . . . as have Fellini, Hitchcock, Huston, and Kurosawa.

Here is a roundup of other *Godfather III* reproofs and reproaches from all over:

"A meandering . . . climax to the saga . . . a slow fuse with a big bang."
—Richard Corliss, *Time*

"Unlike *Godfather* and *Godfather II* it is not a masterpiece. The disappointment can be crushing."
—Jami Bernard, *New York Post*

"The narrative urgency is simply not there anymore. . . ."
—Andrew Sarris, *New York Observer*

"It is flat and uninvolving, and given the material, the budget and the sixteen year wait, it seems—at least to some Godfatherphiles—an infuriating waste of an opportunity. . . . It took a free-fall from the level of perfection reached by its predecessors . . . a disappointing work from a declining genius. . . ."
—Jack Mathews, *Los Angeles Times*

"The faults are . . . worrisome. The editing leaves fissures. . . . Why do so many loud-mouthed antagonists defy the family without learning from previous examples? Why don't they know they're going to be killed? . . . Al Pacino is still hard to credit as Brando's heir; he looks as if Brando could have him for breakfast. . . . And we can only be grateful that Diane Keaton is not on screen any more than she is. . . . Al Pacino plays Michael and plays him somewhat overly stoop-shouldered and antique for a man in his early sixties. This approach doesn't lend much authority to a performance that was never authoritative enough."
—Stanley Kauffman, *New Republic*

CHAPTER 9

The Godfather Comes to Television

IN THE FIFTIES THE ARRIVAL of television slashed movie income, diminished the number of theaters, shortened the careers of movie stars, and halved movie production. Television was the movie's nemesis.

It is therefore ironic that it was a movie that brought people to television in record numbers. NBC paid Paramount ten million dollars for a single two-night airing of *The Godfather,* the greatest sum a network had ever paid a movie studio for television rights to a film. The previous high was five million dollars, the amount NBC paid MGM for a single showing of *Gone With the Wind.* "Nothing's as important as the land," Scarlett O'Hara's father tells her. But with *The Godfather,* nothing was as important as the huge audience it could attract.

Of course, television had its limitations in screen size (which is why 20th Century-Fox created Cinemascope).

NBC had paid MGM $5 million for a single showing of *Gone With the Wind.* It broke that record when it paid Paramount $10 million for a single airing of the original *Godfather.*

The Godfather, and later Godfather II, lost a good deal on the small screen. The television screen forfeited the vital scope and sweep and size of the two films, the sense of the Corleone family spreading its tentacles across the country, from New York to Nevada to Hollywood, and beyond America's shores to Cuba and Sicily.

Television also compromised the visual vastness of the family ceremonies—the weddings, the christenings, and the communions; and it lost some of the grim quality of the deep-brown paneling and menacing shadows of the Corleone offices, where murders were planned and annihilations plotted.

The movie also lost some important details to NBC's Standards and Practices Department (less euphemistically, its censors). They felt that certain scenes in The Godfather might corrupt their viewers and did not adhere to "community standards." Their cuts included a shot of Apollonia's naked breasts on her wedding night with Michael and the scene where Sonny puts Lucy against the wall for a hurried coupling as Tom Hagen calls, "The old man wants to see you." Another trim was demanded in the scene where Sonny

The Godfather—as you've never seen it!

Starting tonight—and continuing for the next three nights—NBC will broadcast "Mario Puzo's The Godfather: The Complete Novel for Television." For the first time viewers will have the opportunity to see the Godfather story told in chronological order. The keystone of the nine hour presentation will be the first television showing of "Godfather II" plus important film never-before-seen on any screen!

All the magnificent drama of the Academy Award-winning motion pictures (nine Oscars), the brilliantly-etched characters, the rich settings and the inspired performances of Marlon Brando, Al Pacino, Robert DeNiro, Diane Keaton, James Caan, Robert Duvall, Talia Shire, Abe Vigoda and Lee Strasberg are preserved and enhanced in this unique television event.

The entire production has been personally — and masterfully — reshaped for television by the man who directed and co-authored, with Puzo, the screenplays for both "Godfather" movies, Francis Ford Coppola. He has been able in this new form to achieve a sense of continuity and scope that simply could not be realized in a theatrical presentation.

It starts tonight at 9 PM!

4N

A COPPOLA COMPANY PRODUCTION   PARENTAL DISCRETION ADVISED

beats up Carlo in the street for blackening his sister's eye. The scene was brutally realistic: Jimmy Caan broke a couple of the actor's ribs. Another cut eliminated the sight of the killers kicking Sonny's supine corpse after they've machine-gunned him to death at the highway tollbooths, and the censors

also trimmed the image of blood dripping from casino owner Moe Greene's face after he has been shot through the eye on the massage table.

As to The Godfather's felonies, add the crime of extortion to gambling, union corruption, and prostitution. NBC extorted big money

Chapter 2..."The Godfather: The Complete Novel for TV"

9PM

Marlon Brando
Al Pacino
Robert DeNiro
Diane Keaton
James Caan
Robert Duvall

Chapters 3 & 4
tomorrow & Tuesday.

Parental discretion advised.

4 N

With film never before shown anywhere!

A Coppola Company Production

Chapter 3..."The Godfather: The Complete Novel for TV"

9PM

Marlon Brando
Al Pacino
Robert DeNiro
Diane Keaton
James Caan
Robert Duvall

The final chapter begins at 8 PM tomorrow!

Parental discretion advised.

4 N

With film never before shown anywhere!

A Coppola Company Production

from advertisers for the chance to have their message shown at the commercial breaks. The network charged advertisers $250,000 per minute for the twenty-eight minutes of commercials—which broke the then current Super Bowl record of $215,000. Although ad revenue never reached the amount paid to Paramount, sing no sad songs for NBC. The film was shown during "sweeps" week, when audience size is measured so the network can set advertising rates for upcoming months. And the number of viewers drawn by *The Godfather* set elevated rates.

Paramount, of course, had the ten million dollars for the two-night stand, plus a magnificent "trailer" for their second *Godfather* film which, not coincidentally, was scheduled to open one month later. Ninety million viewers watched this trailer for *The Godfather, Part II*: 38 percent of all the television sets in America that were turned on were tuned to *The Godfather*. It became the fourth most popular movie in the history of television, in the wake of *Love Story, Airport,* and *The Poseidon Adventure*. These three films, whatever their appeal, lacked *The Godfather*'s underpinning as social history. (John Marley, whose daughter had died in *Love Story,* showed up with a horse's head in his bed in *The Godfather*.)

Tallulah Bankhead once described television as, "like being shot out of a cannon. Someone lights a fuse and BANG—there you are in someone's living room." *The Godfather* created quite a BANG. The airing of the first segment was viewed by 6,500,000 people in New York City alone. (Compare this to the one million people nationwide who bought the "runaway bestseller" in hardcover.) When the second half of the film was aired it drew seven million viewers in New

The original airing of *The Godfather* was viewed by seven million people in New York. It drained the night life out of Manhattan, a record for TV movie watching in the Big Apple.

Surface streets of Manhattan were clogged with traffic as people hurried home to watch *The Godfather*. Patronage at New York's most popular restaurants was down significantly.

York, a record for television movie watching in the Big Apple. (That same evening only 700,000 watched the Chiefs and the Broncos lock horns on "Monday Night Football." When you pit Marlon Brando against Howard Cosell, there is no contest.

Nightlife in Manhattan was brought to a standstill. According to an article in the *New Yorker,* the streets of Manhattan were clogged with traffic, as citizens of the metropolis hurried home to wolf down dinner, in order to watch a film that most of them had already seen in the theaters. Once the film began to roll, traffic no longer did. During the two-hour showing, police reported that traffic was as meager as on Christmas night. Patronage of New York's most popular eateries —from Elaine's to the Rainbow Grill—was way off. When Clemenza showed Michael how to cook for twenty men, the chefs around town had nothing to do but watch him.

Three years later, in the winter of 1977, Francis Ford Coppola's hope that someday the two *Godfather* films might be united was fulfilled. When *The Godfather* was shown on television three years before, it was among the most watched films in television history. When the sequel appeared, featuring many of the same actors, to the powers who rule television it seemed quite sensible to think of a tandem broadcast. Charles Bluhdorn, board chairman of Gulf + Western, talked on the phone to Herb Schlosser, president of NBC. His suggestion was: How about presenting both *Godfathers* together? Schlosser bought the idea and sealed the agreement over the phone.

This time the network paid fifteen million dollars to Paramount for the privilege of bringing the Corleone clan into America's living rooms. The five million dollar increase for two films marked a sizable discount on *Godfather, Part II,* with Coppola's conceptual and editorial genius thrown into the package.

The marriage of the two films could be a thorny business. Who but Francis Coppola could be relied on to ensure the quality and fidelity of the multi-part movie? Thus, part of the deal required the director to personally supervise the new film. He was also committed to restore a significant amount of footage that had been shot but unused.

Unfortunately, Coppola is a man whose attention fixes on one project at a time

'THE GODFATHER' IS REBORN

In a Philippine jungle Francis Ford Coppola turned two movies into nine hours of television

By Edwin Kiester Jr.

Deep in a Philippine jungle, two men are seated on the wide veranda of a low-roofed, white-painted resort cottage. Palm fronds rustle gently against the screens, and mango and papaya trees groan heavily under their fruit. If you listen closely, you can hear the distant rumble of a waterfall. But the tall, bearded American and his companion are oblivious to the romantic setting. Their attention is riveted to the flickering blue-white images on a television set. Occasionally one man will push a button on a tape deck that stops the projection, while the other takes notes. Then the puffy face of Marlon Brando in his Academy Award-winning role of Don Vito Corleone, the Godfather, fills the screen once more . . .

A tropical clearing on the other side of the world may seem an unlikely place to assemble an American tele-

Francis Coppola took time out from the tempestuous filming of *Apocalypse Now* in the Philippines jungle to edit *Godfather I* and *II* for television.

with an almost maniacal dedication to that project. And he was now into another motion picture, *Apocalypse Now.* The movie required all his attention and a great deal of his money. The fine documentary, *Hearts of Darkness,* made by Coppola's wife, Eleanor, showed the disruptive effects of a typhoon that interrupted

shooting. If it weren't for that act of God, *The Godfather Saga* might never have reached television. The storm ravaged the movie company's location, shattering sets and halting production. It may be possible to fight a war under these conditions, but it was impossible to shoot a film. Coppola sent his cast and crew back to the States until mother nature was more hospitable.

One of the crew dispatched stateside was Barry Malkin, the *Apocalypse Now* film editor. He was a boyhood friend of Coppola's and served as a film editor on the second *Godfather* epic. He seemed the right one to take on the television project. Before Coppola returned to the South Pacific, he and Malkin met in Coppola's San Francisco office and mapped the campaign for the television presentation. He not only left his heart in San Francisco, he also left his plans for *The Godfather Saga*.

The first part of the job was an awesome one: to assemble all the materials from the two movies, both the films and the residue in the vaults. Malkin wanted every foot of film that had ever passed through Coppola's camera, and that was a lot. The discarded film, in storage at Paramount for between three and five years, included "trims" (segments of scenes that had been discarded) and "lifts" (whole scenes that were not included in the final film).

Literally hundreds of cartons were dispatched by Paramount to editor Malkin. Every single frame of film that had ever been shot, and

every inch of sound tape that had ever been recorded, descended on him. One entire storeroom in his Manhattan studio was packed with the film. Now, how to assemble it?

In retrospect, the obvious course would be to assemble it in chronological order. But this was by no means clear at the time. After all, there were three distinct time periods covered by the two films:

(1) the early 1900's when the young Don fights to escape the perils of Sicily and then, as an immigrant in New York, confronts the Black Hand,

(2) the period in the mid-Forties when Don Vito is at the height of his power and head of one of the Five Families that rule organized crime in America, and

(3) the Fifties when the fate of the family is in the hands of Michael Corleone and he is mapping out new terrain in Las Vegas and Havana.

Coppola reflected that there were numerous ways he could proceed. He could do flashbacks and flash-forwards, an approach he handled adroitly in the second film. He could draw parallels and show analogies in the lives of

the three Corleone generations. Or then again he could. . . .

But it seemed sensible, as a first step, to put the storeroom of film into chronological order. Thus, he would begin with the Sicily scenes, flow forward through the action in Little Italy, and then move to the events in Nevada and finally in Cuba. All the abandoned footage would be woven into this framework.

There had been many reasons why the trims and lifts had been left on the cutting room floor, most of them involving directorial judgment. Some of the scenes were very good, some were of dubious merit. But at this stage, the film editor reinstated everything. Vietnam had its search-and-destroy missions; this mission was search-and-restore.

After all the material had been reinserted, Coppola discovered that he had a film lasting nine and a half hours. It occupied two ceiling-high racks in Malkin's studio; there were fifty-five cans of film and fifty-five cans of sound. It called for a prodigious amount of organization and scrupulous attention to detail.

The assiduous process took three months and—lo and behold—the director discovered that the

Mario Puzo's
The Godfather Saga
THE COMPLETE NOVEL FOR TELEVISION

DeNiro! Brando!

9 Academy Awards! Here is the monumental Godfather saga—"The Godfather" and "The Godfather Part II"—with exciting scenes never shown in motion picture theatres. **4 Great Nights!**   A COPPOLA COMPANY PRODUCTION

Caan! Pacino!

Al Pacino as Michael Corleone | James Caan as Sonny Corleone | Marlon Brando as Don Vito Corleone | Diane Keaton as Kay Adams | Robert DeNiro as the young Vito Corleone

Robert Duvall as Tom Hagen | Talia Shire as Connie Rizzi | Abe Vigoda as Tessio | Lee Strasberg as Hyman Roth

8:00 PM
4
PARENTAL DISCRETION ADVISED

NBC broadcast the first two *Godfather* films in a nine-hour form that stretched over four evenings. Coppola re-edited the two films into chronological order.

chronological structure, which he had undertaken simply as a jumping-off point, worked remarkably well! It was proving an effective way to turn two movies into four evenings of television, and maintain both narrative thrust and viewer impact.

Some critics were negative about the chronological format. The restructuring meant that the flashbacks no longer occurred as *flashbacks* but as events in the present. Some found this objectionable. Molly Haskell, writing in *The Village Voice,* found it "self-contradictory, like trying to straighten out a pretzel." She pointed out, for example, that the Little Italy sequences, in which

Robert De Niro plays the young Vito, were shot to have "the fragmentary, carefully-framed look of images seen through the telescope of memory." Now they were no longer flashbacks, yet they retained a nostalgic image.

With Coppola still fighting the Vietnam War in the Philippines, editor Malkin transferred the film to half-inch videotape, the kind used in VCRs. He inserted a running-time code so that he could promptly locate any frame that needed alteration. The conversion to half-inch tape diminished the huge assembly to only nine cassettes, less than you'd need for a home library of the films of John Wayne. The film editor

sent them to Coppola in the windswept Philippines. Coppola wasted little time in wading through the nine cassettes, giving it his imprimatur, and getting the okay from NBC and Paramount to take the next step.

Fortunately, there was another break in filming, and Coppola and Malkin met again in California. Their aim was to divide the film into three two-hour segments and one three-hour segment. Each two-hour segment required seven acts; the three-hour one required eleven acts. The break points could not be chosen lightly. Coppola had to select a dramatic moment in the show for each interruption, so viewers would not tune out. Naturally, the overall length had to allow time for commercials so the film had to be cut by roughly two hours. (It's business, Sonny, it's not personal.)

It is intriguing to observe the scenes that were restored in its multi-evening presentation, for it shows the high quality of the material that gets trimmed from a great film in order to quicken its pace. The director is like a ship's captain, throwing things overboard in order to pick up speed. One of the restored scenes showed Don Corleone listening to Tom Hagen report on the failure of his mission to convince producer Woltz to give Johnny Fontane a role in the career-making movie.

Also reinstated was a scene of Vito killing two bodyguards who had been involved in the murder of his father. And Coppola further restored the scene in which Michael has his revenge on Fabrizio, the bodyguard who betrayed him and inadvertently killed his wife. The television viewer also sees the discarded scene of Michael in the hills of Sicily, talking to his bodyguards, plus a sequence of a child star and her mother looking on as Woltz orders Tom Hagen from his home.

Once more the director

headed for the Philippines and his search for Colonel Kurtz. He kept his set of videotapes on location and whenever he cried "cut" on a scene in *Apocalypse Now,* he would direct his attention from Vietnam to Staten Island and the Corleone compound. (Robert Duvall, who he was directing as a Marine Major in the Philippines, became a *consiglieri* on the tape.) As Coppola did his work, Malkin risked malaria to fly in and join him. He arrived as Coppola was filming an assault by American troops on the Philippine river that was doubling for the Mekong Delta. The director and the film editor worked without sleep on a final cut, until it was ready for the airwaves.

NBC was a little worried. (It is in the nature of television networks to worry.) After the violence and rage of the Sixties, 1977 was a year when America was settling into a more moderate mode with Jimmy Carter at the helm. But *The Godfather* films were undeniably two of the most graphically ferocious films anyone had seen in a long time, and their dialogue was explicit. In 1974, Coppola had needed to launder *The Godfather* for its initial showing; three years later there was even less

broadcasting freedom. NBC told its head of Broadcast Standards to review the shows with a sharp eye.

Coppola had no desire to offend the viewers, but he was anxious to keep the dynamics of his narrative. Whenever he removed a piece of dialogue, he insisted that it be replaced by something just as good. So sound crews fanned out across Hollywood and New York to round up members of the original *Godfather* cast. Robert De Niro, Lee Strasberg, and others were hounded down to tape the substitute lines. They had played a lot of parts since their *Godfather* days, and it was not easy to find their way back into the attitude of their Mafia roles.

After the NBC censors had their way with the composite film, here are a few of the moments that had been laundered for home viewing:

- The episode in which De Niro returns to Sicily and avenges his father's murder was truncated so that he only thrusts a knife toward his victim. He does not stab and twist it.

- The well-loved horse's head scene was trimmed.

- Blood did not spurt from Sonny's body when he is

gunned down by Barzini's gang.

NBC wanted Francis Coppola to film a brief introduction to the series, but he passed on the request. He was now deeply involved in *Apocalypse Now* and could spare no more time. For the network, the introduction was important. There were those who would protest the film's implied insult to Italian-Americans, and there were those who would object to the violence on television. NBC could not ignore these outspoken partisans and wanted to protect both its flanks. So they taped the introduction with the director's sister, Talia Shire.

The actress explained to possibly irate viewers that the movies were, of course, fiction. Said Shire, They "detail the frightening actions of a small criminal group and it would be grossly unfair to let these characterizations and their story represent the deeds of Italians. . . ." She added, "This is not the story of an entire people whose contributions are tremendously valued by us all."

In addition to the Shire explanation, NBC also prepared cards full of text that appeared on the air along with a voice-over so it could be both read and heard. The

cards were run every night before the show began and again before the start of the second act. They restated much of what Talia Shire had said.

NBC also aired a warning about violence to placate those who found too much of it in television. It emphasized that the film was a "classic" and that the criminals earned retribution. The warning read, "This motion picture classic presents a realistic depiction of the self-destructive effects of crime and violence, and though it has been edited for television, parental discretion is advised."

Despite NBC's wariness, UNICO National, America's largest Italian-American service organization with 200 chapters in the U.S. and a membership of 12,000, called for a "nationwide blackout" of the televised *Godfather*. They asked viewers to keep their sets dark. UNICO also planned demonstrations in front of NBC's offices and studios. Despite the flattering presentation of the Mafia in *The Godfather,* the Italian-American community was still angry about the epic. However, most agreed with historian Arthur Schlesinger that, given the glamourized, glorified presentation of the underworld, rather than protest the screening, the

organization should have financed it.

When NBC presented Coppola's two extraordinary films in tandem, they called it *The Godfather Saga: The Complete Novel for Television*— not a strictly accurate title, as many of the events in the second film were not in the novel at all, but were invented for the movie by Puzo and Coppola. To the television audience, the *Saga* presented Coppola's best effort to unite the two movies, each of which had won the Academy Award for Best Picture. They formed one continuous narrative and proved both an artistic and a commercial triumph. If there were an award for conceptual dexterity and victory over technical impediments, Coppola would have won that one too.

Television has always had its critics. As the news executive said in Paddy Chayefsky's *Network,* "Television is not the truth. Television is a goddam amusement park . . . we're in the boredom-killing business." On the evenings when it brought *The Godfather Saga* to the public, television was far more than an amusement park or a boredom-killer. It reflected one of the most remarkable achievements of the motion-picture industry.

CHAPTER 10

The Quotable Corleones

STEVEN SPIELBERG, THE master of the action film, said recently, "It's time we got back to the words." He meant that what draws us to the movies today is special effects, car chases, and high-concept plots—not the dialogue. But, because director Francis Coppola is an Oscar-winning screenwriter and Mario Puzo is a talented novelist, the words are very good in *The Godfather*. This is not the primitive dialogue of a *Rocky* or a *Dirty Harry*, where the height of eloquence is "Go for it," "Make my day," or "Read my lips." It is not a *Terminator 2* where the most memorable line is, "Hasta la vista, baby."

Memorable lines do not usually abound in gangster films. *The Godfather* is a notable exception. There are a number of lines that instantly bring memories of the scenes and circumstances in which they were spoken. Here are some of the most memorable words from the *Godfather Saga*.

FROM
THE GODFATHER

"I'm gonna make him an offer he can't refuse."

—Don Corleone to Johnny Fontane about Woltz

"Mr. Corleone is a man who insists on hearing bad news immediately."

—Tom Hagen to Woltz

"My father taught me many things . . . keep your friends close, but your enemies closer."

—Michael to Pentangeli

"If history has taught us anything, it's that you can kill anybody."

—Michael to Tom Hagen

"No Sicilian can refuse any request on his daughter's wedding day."

—Tom Hagen to his wife

"Certainly, he can present a bill for such services. We're not Communists, after all. But he has to let us draw water from the well."

—Barzini to the other Dons

"Never let anyone outside the family know what you're thinking again."

—Don Corleone to Sonny

"Some day, and that day may never come, I may ask a service of you."

—Don Corleone to Bonasera

"Leave the gun. Take the cannolis."

—Clemenza to Rocco

"I don't want my brother coming out of that toilet with just his dick in his hand."

—Sonny to Tom Hagen

"Don't ever take sides with anyone against the family again."

—Michael to Fredo

"A man who doesn't spend time with his family can never be a real man."

—Don Corleone to Johnny Fontane

"Luca Brasi sleeps with the fishes."

—Clemenza to Sonny

"Mr. Corleone is Johnny's godfather. To the Italian people, that is a very religious, sacred, close relationship."

— Tom Hagen to Woltz

"Look at that spooky looking guy."

— Kay to Michael about Luca Brasi

"I am a superstitious man. And if some unlucky accident should befall my son . . . if my son is struck by a bolt of lightning, I will blame some of the people here."

— Don Corleone to the other Dons

"You gotta go, you gotta go."

— McCluskey granting Michael permission to go to the bathroom

"Don Corleone, I am honored and grateful that you have invited me to your home on the wedding day of your daughter. May their first child be a masculine child."

— Luca Brasi to Don Corleone

"I guess I'm getting too old for my job. Too grouchy. Can't stand the aggravation."

— McCluskey to Michael

"Do you know who I am? I'm Moe Greene, and I made my bones while you were going out with cheerleaders."

— Moe Greene to Michael

"Luca Brasi held a gun to [the band leader's] head and my father assured him that either his brains or his signature would be on the contract."

— Michael to Kay

FROM
THE GODFATHER, PART II

"We're all part of the same hypocrisy, Senator. But never think it applies to my family."

— Michael to Senator Geary

"I know it was you, Fredo. You broke my heart."

— Michael to Fredo

"I loved baseball ever since Arnold Rothstein fixed the World Series in 1919."

— Hyman Roth to Michael

"But Vito is only nine. And dumb-witted. The child cannot harm you."

— Vito's mother to Don Ciccio

"Hyman Roth always makes money for his partners."

— Johnny Ola to Michael

"I don't like your kind of people. I don't like to see you come out to this clean country in oily hair and dressed up in those silk suits, and try to pass yourselves off as decent Americans."

— Senator Geary to Michael

"It wasn't a miscarriage. It was an abortion. Like our marriage is an abortion."

— Kay to Michael

"This truck you hijacked was in my neighborhood. You should let me wet my beak a little."

—Fanucci to Vito

"Michael, we're bigger than U.S. Steel!"

—Hyman Roth to Michael

"Mike, I'm your older brother. I was stepped over."

—Fredo to Michael

"I'm going to take a nap. When I wake up, if the money is on the table, I'll know I have a partner. If it isn't, I'll know I don't."

—Hyman Roth to Michael

"Yeah, a buffer. The family had a lot of buffer."

—Willy Cicci to the Senate Committee

"Good health is the most important thing. More than success, more than money, more than power."

—Hyman Roth to Michael

"You're nothing to me now, Fredo, not a brother, not a friend. . . . When you visit our mother, I want to know a day in advance. So I won't be there."

—Michael to Fredo

"I don't trust a doctor who can hardly speak English."

—Hyman Roth to Mobster

"Where's Michael? I've got things to get straight with him and I can't wait on line."

—Connie to Mama Corleone

"They went home and sat in a hot bath and opened their veins, and bled to death."

—Pentangeli to Tom Hagen

"Every time I put the line down I would say a Hail Mary, and every time I said a Hail Mary, I would catch a fish.

—Fredo to Anthony

"You give your loyalty to a Jew over your own blood."

—Pentangeli to Michael

"I am a retired investor on a pension, and I wished to live there as a Jew in the twilight of my life."

—Hyman Roth to reporters

"A kid comes up to me in a white jacket, gives me a Ritz cracker and chopped liver, he says 'Canapes,' I say, 'Can o' peas my ass: that's a Ritz cracker and chopped liver.' "

—Pentangeli to Fredo

"I didn't ask who gave the order, because it had nothing to do with business."

—Hyman Roth to Michael

"What's with him? I gotta get a letter of introduction to have a 'sitdown'?"

—Pentangeli to Fredo

"I dislike dogs myself."

—Vito to Landlord

"When pop had troubles, did he ever think that maybe by trying to be strong, and trying to protect his family, that he could lose it instead?"

—Michael to Mama Corleone

"I knew there would be no way you could ever forgive me, not with this Sicilian thing that goes back two thousand years."

—Kay to Michael

"It would be a shame if a few rotten apples spoiled the whole barrel."

—Senator Geary at Michael's hearing

"Can't you forgive Fredo? He's so sweet and helpless."

—Connie to Michael

"Hyman Roth will never see the new year."

—Michael to Fredo

"You know, now that you're so respectable, Michael, you're more dangerous than you were. I think I preferred you when you were just a common Mafia hood."

—Kay to Michael

"I'll always be your son, but I will never have anything to do with your business."

—Anthony to Michael

"In today's world, it seems the power to absolve debt is greater than the power of forgiveness."

—The Archbishop to Michael

"I've lost all the venom, all the juice of youth. I've lost all the lust for women and now my mind is clear."

—Don Altobello to Michael

"Do I have to see him?"

—Michael referring to Joey Zasa

"My nephew is a nice boy, but he talks when he should be listening."

—Michael referring to Vincent

"I want you to sell your soul to Don Altobello. To betray me."

—Michael to Vincent

"Call a meeting . . . we will have the peace."

—Michael to Don Altobello

CHAPTER 11

Timetable

Mᴏʀᴇ ᴛʜᴀɴ ᴀ ᴍᴇʀᴇ gangster film, the *Godfather* movies offered us a social history. There was an intense reality to the events in *The Godfather Saga* that moviegoers found riveting. To gain more perspective about the times in which the movies' events occurred, many filmgoers found themselves asking, "What was happening in the real world while these things were happening to the Corleones?"

Against the background of brutality and murder in the Corleone family one can see the unfolding brutality and murder in the world of international relations. In the film *Monsieur Verdoux,* Charles Chaplin has his bluebeard say, "One murder makes a villain, millions a hero." This comparison of individual and national crime also appears in *The Godfather,* when Michael defends his family by saying that his father does nothing that

other powerful men, like presidents, don't do. Kay accuses Michael of being naive and adds, "Presidents don't have men killed," to which Michael replies, "Now who's being naive?"

A Mafia family offers the vast world in microcosm, but an extremely tight little world. Here is a timetable of what was happening beyond that tight little world—in the wide and equally tumultuous world outside.

1908 *Vito Marries*

Earthquake in Sicily kills 150,000
Wright Brothers demonstrate their airplane to the U.S. Government
U.S. Army buys its first aircraft, a dirigible
Union of South Africa is established
Lyndon B. Johnson, future President, is born
Ian Fleming, creator of James Bond, is born
Jack Johnson becomes first black heavyweight boxing champ
General Motors is formed
Baseball rules the spitball illegal
The fountain pen is invented
The Ford Motor Company produces the first Model T

1915 *The Little Italy sequence begins*

First German submarine attack in World War I
W. Somerset Maugham writes *Of Human Bondage*
Arthur Miller, future playwright, is born
D. W. Griffith's *Birth of a Nation* is released
Albert Einstein postulates his Theory of Relativity
Henry Ford develops the tractor
Congress establishes the Coast Guard
Margaret Sanger is jailed for writing book on birth control
President Woodrow Wilson gets married
Motorized taxis appear
Auto speed record of 102 m.p.h. is set

1916 *Sonny Corleone is born*

Gas masks and steel helmets introduced in German army

Italy declares war on Germany

Lawrence of Arabia appointed liaison to Faisal's army

Woodrow Wilson re-elected President

Pancho Villa and his army cross American border

Louis Brandeis named to U.S. Supreme Court

Prohibition gains ground, twenty-four states vote against alcohol

First Rose Bowl game is played

Boston Red Sox defeat Brooklyn Dodgers in World Series

1919 *Vito kills Fanucci of the Black Hand*

The "Black Sox" bribery scandal rocks baseball

Prohibition amendment to the Constitution ratified

Benito Mussolini founds Fascist party in Italy

German peace treaty signed at Versailles

The Prince of Wales tours America

Woodrow Wilson wins the Nobel Peace Prize

First experiments with shortwave radio

Jack Dempsey wins the heavyweight boxing championship

The American Legion is formed

The mechanical rabbit is invented for greyhound racing

1920 *Vito intervenes with the landlord on behalf of woman with dog*

Anarchists Sacco and Vanzetti arrested

Bomb explodes on Wall Street

League of Nations opens in Paris

Senate defeats membership in League of Nations

Republicans nominate Warren Harding and Calvin Coolidge

Women vote for the first time in a national election

Democrats nominate Franklin Roosevelt for Vice President

1923 *Connie Corleone is born*

Minimum wage for women declared unconstitutional

President Harding dies of cerebral apoplexy

Economy soars, unemployment falls

John D. Rockefeller pays $7.4 million in taxes

Ku Klux Klan Convention draws 200,000

Pancho Villa is assassinated

Adolf Hitler fails to overthrow German government

Senate starts Teapot Dome investigation

1925 *Vito kills Don Ciccio in Italy*

Leon Trotsky is demoted, Joseph Stalin
extends power

World powers sign treaty to outlaw poison
gas

John Scopes goes on trial for teaching
evolution

Billy Mitchell is court–martialed for
insubordination

Florida land scams are exposed, lots that
are underwater are sold

1941 *The Don's birthday party*

Germany invades Russia

FDR embargoes oil and scrap metal to
Japan

FDR and Churchill meet in North
Atlantic

Germans reach outskirts of Leningrad,
threaten Moscow

Hideki Tojo becomes Japanese premier

Japanese attack Pearl Harbor in surprise air
assault

Germany and Italy declare war on U.S.

Wake Island and Guam fall to the Japanese

Draft is extended, men 18–65 must
register

Germans send army under Rommel to
Africa to fight British

1945 *Don Corleone is gunned down*

1,000 plane armadas bomb Germany

FDR, Churchill, Stalin meet at Yalta

Iwo Jima is captured and flag raised on
Mount Suribachi

FDR dies of cerebral hemorrhage

Buchenwald is liberated

Mussolini and mistress are executed in
Milan

Hitler commits suicide

Germany surrenders unconditionally

First atom bomb is tested in New Mexico

Truman, Churchill, Stalin meet at Potsdam

Atom bomb is dropped on Hiroshima,
189,000 casualties

Atom bomb is dropped on Nagasaki

Japanese surrender unconditionally

1946 *Michael is exiled to Sicily*

Twelve nazis sentenced to death at
　　Nuremberg
Juan Peron elected President of Argentina
Civil War rages in China
First U.N. meeting held in London
Fair Employment Practices Act is defeated
　　in Senate
Korean government set up, USSR controls
　　north, U.S. controls south
Truman orders railroads seized if workers
　　strike

1947 *Michael returns from Sicily and the Five Families War begins*

Truman orders loyalty oaths for all federal
　　employees
Truman Doctrine provides support to
　　Greece and Turkey
HUAC begins hearings on Hollywood
　　Communists
Henry Wallace announces candidacy for
　　President
Palestine question goes before U.N.
George Marshall proposes plan to help
　　rebuild Europe

1948 *Sonny is killed*

Mahatma Gandhi is assassinated
Tojo and five others hang for war crimes
Russia bans land traffic to Berlin, West
　　airlifts supplies
Truman defeats Dewey in giant upset

Israel is created by U.N.

1949 *Michael makes Moe Greene an offer for his casino*

U.S. recognizes Israel
Whittaker Chambers accuses Alger Hiss of
　　spying
North Atlantic Pact is signed and NATO
　　created
Berlin blockade is lifted
Communists drive nationalists off mainland
　　of China

Last U.S. troops leave Korea

Apartheid begins in South Africa

1951 *Michael and Kay marry*

Ethel and Julius Rosenberg are sentenced
　　to death
U.S. tests A-bomb near Las Vegas

U.S. will send 100,000 troops to Europe
Truman says Russia seeks world conquest
22d Amendment limits president to two
    terms
Truman relieves Douglas MacArthur
Cease-fire talks reopen in Panmunjom

1954 *The Don dies*

Sam Sheppard is accused of his wife's
    murder
Joseph McCarthy probe of army begins
Gamal Abdel Nasser becomes premier of
    Egypt
Army charges McCarthy and Cohn sought
    favors for Schine
Senate hearings on army-McCarthy
    dispute begin
French fortress at Dien Bien Phu,
    Vietnam, falls
Supreme Court rules school segregation
    unconstitutional
British agree to return Suez Canal to
    Egypt

1955 *Michael has heads of Five Families executed*

Military ousts Juan Peron
Nikita Khrushchev becomes party
    secretary
Ike suffers heart attack
James Dean dies in car crash
AFL and CIO merge
U.S. begins aid to Indochina
General Motors splits 3 for 1

1958 *Anthony's first communion celebration*

Alaska is admitted to the union
Chinese bombard Quemoy and Matsu
Sherman Adams resigns over bribe of
    vicuna coat
Castro-led rebels seize provincial capital of
    Cuba
Pope Pius XII dies

Vice President Nixon is stoned in Caracas,
Venezuela

Charles de Gaulle becomes French premier

One-and-a-half ton Sputkik III orbits
Mao Tse-Tung and Khrushchev parley in
    Peking

1959 *Michael is in Havana*

Khrushchev boasts of Soviet military
    superiority
Hawaii becomes the fiftieth state
Castro visits U.S. and is warmly received
Charles Van Doren admits his television
    quiz was fixed
Nixon, on Russian television, asks
    Russians to improve
Laos asks for U.S. aid against aggression by
    Vietnam

Fidel Castro takes Havana, Batista flees

Two monkeys are recovered after orbit

Khrushchev tours the U.S.

1975 *Michael decides to divest himself of criminal holdings*

Lynette "Squeaky" Fromme arrested for
    pointing gun at President Ford
Patty Hearst is arrested by FBI
CIA acknowledges plots to kill heads of
    state
Saigon falls to North Vietnam
Massive death toll feared in Cambodia

Haldeman, Ehrlichman, Mitchell convicted
    of conspiracy

Jimmy Hoffa disappears, foul play
    suspected

Israel and Egypt sign Sinai agreement

1979 *Anthony makes his debut*

Lord Mountbatten is assassinated in Ireland
Students seize embassy in Iran, sixty-two
   Americans held hostage
Vietnam takes over Cambodia
OPEC announces further oil–price raise
One and a half billion dollar federal
   bailout loan to Chrysler

Accident at Three Mile Island nuclear
   plant

U.S. and China establish diplomatic
   relations

Margaret Thatcher elected, first female
   Prime Minister in Britain

U.S. and Russia complete Salt II
   agreement

Russia invades Afghanistan

CHAPTER 12

The Great Actor Returns

WINSTON CHURCHILL, referring to the years when Britain failed to arm despite Hitler's threat, said, "These are the years the locusts have eaten." With his appearance in *The Godfather* in 1972, Marlon Brando could look back on a decade that the locusts had eaten. He reached the end of the longest period a major American actor has gone through without a resounding critical or commercial success. From 1960 through 1971 he had appeared in a series of films for which his fans wept. Michael Medved, author of *The Golden Turkey Awards,* might well have produced a companion volume based on the Brando films of the Sixties. They were:

1960

The Fugitive Kind, from a play by Tennessee Williams, directed by Sidney Lumet, a United Artists release.

1961

One Eyed Jacks, a revenge Western, starring and directed by Brando, a Paramount release.

1962

Mutiny on the Bounty, a remake of the classic 1935 film, co-starring Trevor Howard, an MGM release.

1963

The Ugly American, based on the successful novel, directed by George Englund, a Universal release.

1964

Bedtime Story, a sex comedy written by Stanley Shapiro, co-starring David Niven, a Universal release.

1965

Morituri, a thriller, co-starring Yul Brynner and Trevor Howard, a 20th Century-Fox release.

1966

The Chase, a film of racial violence, written by Lillian Hellman and directed by Arthur Penn, a Columbia release.

1966

The Appaloosa, a Western, directed by Sidney Furie and co-starring John Saxon, a Universal release.

1967

A Countess from Hong Kong, a farcical comedy, directed and written by Charles Chaplin, a Universal release.

1967

Reflections in a Golden Eye, a drama directed by John Huston and co-starring Elizabeth Taylor, a Seven Arts release.

1968

Candy, a dark sex comedy from the novel by Terry Southern, included a cameo performance by Brando, a Selmur release.

1968

Burn!, a drama directed by Gillo Pontecorvo and co-starring Renato Salvatori, a PEA/PPA release.

1969

The Night of the Following Day, a kidnapping adventure, co-starring Richard Boone and Rita Moreno, a Universal release.

1971

The Nightcomers, a prequel to *The Turn of the Screw* with Brando as Quint, a Kastner-Kantor-Ladd release.

———

Here are reactions to several of the films in which Brando chose to appear in the decade before *The Godfather.*

Mutiny on the Bounty:
Didn't come close to the original. Brando seemed all wrong as Fletcher Christian. Overlong and unattractive remake marred principally by Brando's English accent and various production follies, not to mention his overlong and bloody death scene. After the landing in Tahiti, boredom sets in along with anti-climax.

The Ugly American:
Brando is an American ambassador to an Asian country, and his arrival stirs up pro-communist elements and produces havoc. Not a

very exciting film. The book was muddled and boring, and the film didn't improve on the potboiler.

The Appaloosa:
A cowboy's plan to start a stud farm is interrupted by badmen who think he has molested their girl. It was a mannered, slow western. Brando and his director constantly strove to upstage one another. Brando used beady eyes and a sweaty forehead; the director used eccentric camera angles framed by objects such as cook fires, grillwork, and fingers. Paulene Kael called it "a dog of a movie about a horse."

One Eyed Jacks:
An outlaw has a running battle with an old friend, played by Karl Malden. It was a self-indulgent Western contrived by Brando, full of long, solemn pauses and explosions of excessive violence.

Bedtime Story:
Two Riviera conmen try to outwit each other. Stanley Shapiro, who had written most of the comedies in which Doris Day protects her virginity from Rock Hudson until they reach the altar, seemed to be tiring of the form. Sex comedy was growing smirkier with the

approaching end of film censorship in 1968. The London *Daily Express* called it "the most vulgar and embarrassing film of the year." Steve Martin recently remade the movie as *Dirty Rotten Scoundrels.*

Reflections in a Golden Eye:
John Huston directed an adaptation of the novel by Carson McCullers. Critics attacked it unmercifully. John Simon said, "One feels trapped in a huge, overheated hothouse containing nothing but common snapdragons." Said Judith Crist: "Nothing more than nutty people and pseudo porn."

The Chase:
Brando played a liberal southern sheriff who takes his ritual beating. Rex Reed called it "the worst thing that has happened to movies since Lassie played a war veteran with amnesia." He added, "Considering all the talent connected with it, it is hard to imagine how it went so haywire." (In addition to Brando, the film starred Jane Fonda and Robert Redford; John Huston directed the Lillian Hellman script.)

———

Here was the actor who in *A Streetcar Named Desire, The Wild One,* and *On the*

Waterfront, had reinvented the movie hero in entirely different terms—and assisted an entire generation in "finding itself."

Brando came to maturity during the Fifties, a period when Hollywood was in crisis from the inroads of television, and America was suffering from the threat of the Cold War. And there was another foreign culture that frightened us. It was called "Youth."

During the Fifties, Brando dominated our films. In addition to his triumphs in *Streetcar, Waterfront,* and *Wild One,* he had other successes: *The Men, Viva Zapata, Julius Caesar, Guys and Dolls, Sayonara,* and *The Young Lions.* Nothing could have prepared the public for the series of movies that Paulene Kael labeled "the degradation after success."

Brando's acting seemed to be a reaction against the post-World War II yearning for security. The Brando of the Fifties films had no code, just instincts. Cinema-goers watched him develop from a gangster leader to an outlaw, foreshadowing the role he would later play in *The Godfather.* He was antisocial; he seemed to know that society was horsefeathers. And he was a model to the young because he was strong enough to say, "I'm not

going to take it." There was a sense of ferment and menace in his cinema presence. He played tough kids superlatively well—portraying them with swagger, arrogance, and humor. Like Sonny Corleone, he was explosively dangerous. He had no great "ideas," but he had enormous appeal as a hero.

One of the rebels he played—first on the stage, then on the screen—was the brutish lout, Stanley Kowalski in *Streetcar.* Stanley's suggestion of aggression and turmoil lurking behind his mumbled voice was adapted by many in *The Godfather.*

Brando was our favorite angry young man. When as Terry Malloy in *On the Waterfront,* he said to his brother, "You don't understand. I could have had class, I could have been a contender," he spoke for us all. That was the great wailing of lost hopes. Fredo could have said much the same thing to Michael: I was passed over, I could have been a player.

Then came the terrible Sixties, the lost years, and the films in the listless calendar above. . . .

It is sad when America's greatest actor depreciates the art of acting, as he often does, asserting that, after all,

virtually anyone can act. It is distressing to hear him make light of his own enormous talent and achievements. "This business of being a successful actor," he once said, "what's the point? . . . All right, you're a success. You're accepted, welcomed everywhere. But that's all there is. . . ."

And then came *The Godfather.* And with it, after his decade-long dry spell, Marlon Brando must once more put up with being accepted and welcomed everywhere. Which may be why he retires to his home in Tahiti to work on his autobiography and seldom acts in films. In the twenty years since his triumph in *The Godfather,* and his concurrent triumph that year in *Last Tango in Paris,* here is what Brando has done:

1976

The Missouri Breaks, a flawed western with Jack Nicholson.

1978

Superman, a cameo role as Superman's father on the doomed planet Krypton.

1978

Roots, a cameo appearance as American Nazi leader George Lincoln Rockwell.

1979

Apocalypse Now, a relatively brief appearance at the climax of Coppola's spectacular antiwar film.

1980

The Formula, a few scenes in a thriller based on a Steven Shagan novel about synthetic oil.

1989

A Dry White Season, two short scenes as a cynical lawyer in a film about apartheid.

1990

The Freshman, a satiric sendup of his *Godfather* role as an underworld chief.

1992

Christopher Columbus: The Discovery, a small role as a priest in Warner Brothers' 400th anniversary tribute.

Francis Coppola returned our greatest living actor to the focus of our attention. The Don was a wonderful role, the dangerous center of a vast, violent work. But though *The Godfather* would return him to the public eye, only Brando could keep himself there.

THE GREEN YEARS [1950–1958]

The Men
The Wild One
A Streetcar Named Desire
Guys and Dolls
Viva Zapata
Sayonara
The Young Lions
Teahouse of the August Moon
Julius Caesar

THE LOCUST YEARS [1960–1971]

The Ugly American
The Appaloosa
Reflections in a Golden Eye
Mutiny on the Bounty
Bedtime Story
The Chase

The Men (1950) with Everett Sloane

The Wild One (1954)

A Streetcar Named Desire (1951) with
Vivien Leigh

Guys and Dolls (1955) with Jean
Simmons

Viva Zapata (1951)

Sayonara (1957) with Miyoshi Umeki

The Young Lions (1958)

The Teahouse of the August Moon (1956)

The Ugly American (1963)

Julius Caesar (1953)

The Appaloosa (1966)

Reflections in a Golden Eye (1967)

Mutiny on the Bounty (1962) with Trevor Howard

Bedtime Story (1964) with David Niven

The Chase (1966)

The Last Tango in Paris (1972) with Maria Schneider

CHAPTER 13

The Oscars and the Corleones

MARLON BRANDO'S renaissance was as extraordinary as his eclipse had been. He was nominated for the Academy Award for his performance in *The Godfather,* and he promptly became the odds on favorite to win. Ring Lardner had said, "The race is not always to the swift, but that's how you bet." Although the Oscar is not *always* awarded to the charismatic superstar in the outstanding movie, that's how you bet. Within the industry, there was a strong wish to commemorate Brando's work, and Hollywood also wanted to tell him: Come home, all is forgiven. It was the same signal they sent to Charlie Chaplin and, later, to Ingrid Bergman.

Before the awards ceremony, there was much speculation as to whether Brando would

Sasheen Littlefeather appeared with a statement from Brando refusing the Oscar that had been awarded him for Best Actor.

actually appear. But no one anticipated what happened when his name was announced as winner of the Oscar for Best Actor. They were aware that Marlon was not in his assigned seat (winners are traditionally situated on the aisle so they can get to the mike quickly). When Magic Time arrived, people started to notice he had a stand-in—a young woman named Sasheen Littlefeather. (Her real name was Maria Cruz, and a few years later she would bear still another name: Miss American Vampire.) She arrived late for the Oscar ceremony because she had been waiting as Brando continued to revise his written message. (He had watched the rewriting process often enough with Coppola and Puzo.)

You couldn't miss Miss Littlefeather. She wore glorious tribal regalia. Cornering her, the producer of the Oscar show, who had umpteen things on his mind, asked what she had in mind. She displayed Mr. Brando's 400 word statement. The producer shook his head, proclaimed it much too long. There would be no marathon screeds. Miss Littlefeather had 120 seconds, and after that she would be removed from the stage. This producer was no General Custer.

Miss Littlefeather/Cruz was greeted and interrupted by catcalls and cries of derision. Employing the improvisation skills for which her sponsor was famous, she presented a truncated version of Brando's statement. She spoke of the historic injustices the Indians had suffered and of their slanderous presentation in the movies. (Not in Brando's Westerns: *One Eyed Jacks, The Appaloosa,* and *The Missouri Breaks.*) She concluded, "I hope that I have not intruded upon this evening and that we will in the future meet with love and understanding in our hearts." The assembled moviemakers displayed little love and understanding. There was no applause, and a scattering of boos.

Later, in the press room, Miss Littlefeather read Brando's complete proclamation. It ended, "I . . . do not feel that I can as a citizen of the United States accept an award here tonight. I think awards in this country are inappropriate to be received or given until the condition of the American Indian is drastically altered. If we are not our brother's keeper, at least let us not be his executioner."

The comments from within the movie industry ran the gamut from ice to outrage. Michael Caine said

that if a man felt he had to speak his piece, he should have the nerve to do it himself. Clint Eastwood, presenting the Best Picture Oscar, joked that maybe Brando should dedicate it to "all the cowboys shot in John Ford Westerns." Brando was also attacked by an Italian-American group for hypocrisy. They complained, "Frankly, we see a blatant contradiction between your reasons for refusing the award and your participating in a film that has defamed the Italian-American community."

⸻

Others in the film industry also made statements that reflected their political views. This was the year, with the war raging in Vietnam, that *Hearts and Minds* won the Award for Best Documentary. Its producer, Bert Schneider, a "Young Turk" in the industry, read a message of friendship from a North Vietnamese Communist leader. This provoked Frank Sinatra, often as hot-headed as the fictional Sonny Corleone, to read an impromptu disavowal.

⸻

The story of the Oscar for the Best Musical Score provided an acid note to the proceedings. Nino Rota's *Godfather* score had been

Marlon Brando had often participated in protests which deplored the injustices to the American Indians.

nominated and, as the Mafia might have expressed it, the Academy considered "rubbing it out." They said it wasn't "original" and felt that perhaps it should be disqualified.

This unusual action came about after an Academy screening. Some members claimed that portions of the score were reworks of earlier compositions by the composer. Specifically, a seven-minute section in the love scene was in question. It seems that Rota had used the love theme, heard in the Sicilian scenes, some years earlier in a film called *Fortunella*. Members of the Academy's music branch were asked to decide whether this disqualified the score, and they decided that it did. *The Godfather* score was ruled ineligible. So the

Academy brass decided to reballot to fill the fifth spot. The other scores in contention were for *Ben, Fellini's Roma, The Other,* and *Sleuth.*

———

Oscar night when *Godfather II* was in contention was a triumphant one for Francis Ford Coppola. He had the rare distinction of being in competition with himself. For the first time as far as even the old-timers could recall, one director had two movies nominated for Best Picture: *Godfather II* and *The Conversation.* Coppola was also nominated in both screenwriting categories: for Original Screenplay for *The Conversation* and for Best Screenplay Adaptation From Another Source for *Godfather II.*

And Coppola did the hat trick. *He took the triple crown* for Best Picture, Best Director, and Best Screenplay (with Puzo) for *Godfather II.* On top of that, his father, Carmine, won the Oscar for Best Musical Score.

But there was friction among the Coppola family on that happy night, especially among the women. As Mother Italia recalls it, "Francis was jumping up in the air saying, 'This was the best night in our lives.' Well,

Talia lost that night and she said wryly, 'I'm a girl so you forgot about me.' Then Carmine gave his speech. He said, 'If it wasn't for me he wouldn't be here.' I said to him afterward, 'Gee, Carmine, you did a great job. I hope the labor pains weren't too bad.' "

Coppola's mother continued her agenda of reproach. "Francis said to me, 'If I get another Oscar tonight I'm going to mention you.' So he got the third Oscar and went up there and said, 'I had something I was going to say but I don't remember what it was.' "

The next day a friend, observing Carmine's negligent treatment of his wife in his moment of glory, sent Italia Coppola a sardonic telegram that read, "Is CARMINE COPPOLA A WIDOWER?" Despite these squabbles, Carmine's career was energized by his Academy Award. He received offers to write the musical scores for some high-profile television movies. He also scored most of Francis's future movies.

Talia lost the Best Supporting Actress Oscar to Ingrid Bergman for *Murder on the Orient Express.* Bergman was the sentimental favorite. But the nomination

and the exposure increased the demand for Talia Shire in Hollywood. For the first time she became really "hot", and film offers began to rain in.

Francis Ford Coppola won Oscars for best director and best screenplay (with Mario Puzo) of both *Godfather I* and *II*.

As the producer of *The Godfather,* Al Ruddy triumphantly accepted the Academy Award for Best Picture of 1972.

NOMINATIONS

Best Picture—**Al Ruddy**
(He thanked Bob Evans and Peter Bart, but not Coppola!)

Best Actor—**Marlon Brando**

Best Director—**Francis Coppola**

Best Screenplay Adaptation—**Francis Coppola and
Mario Puzo**

Best Editing—**William Reynolds and Peter Zinner**

Best Costume Design—**Anna Hill Johnstone**

Best Sound—**Brad Grenzbach, Richard Portman,
Chris Newman**

Best Supporting Actor—**James Caan, Robert Duvall,
Al Pacino**

Best Musical Score—**Nino Rota**
(The nomination was withdrawn.)

OSCARS WON: THREE
(1) Best Picture
(2) Best Screenplay Adaptation
(3) Best Actor

COMBINED NOMINATIONS FOR *GODFATHER I* AND *II:* TWENTY

COMBINED OSCARS WON BY *GODFATHER I* AND *II:* NINE

COMBINED NOMINATIONS FOR *GODFATHER I, II,* AND *III:* TWENTY-SEVEN

COMBINED OSCARS FOR *GODFATHER I, II,* AND *III:* NINE

OSCAR SCORECARD—
THE GODFATHER, PART II (1974)

NOMINATIONS

Best Picture—**Francis Coppola**

Best Director—**Francis Coppola**

Best Screenplay Adaptation—**Francis Coppola and Mario Puzo**

Best Actor—**Al Pacino**

Best Supporting Actress—**Talia Shire**

Best Supporting Actor—**Robert De Niro, Lee Strasberg, Michael Gazzo**

Best Musical Score—**Nino Rota and Carmine Coppola**

Best Art Direction—**Dean Tavoularis and Angelo Graham**

Best Costumes—**Theadore Von Runkle**

OSCARS WON: SIX
(1) Best Picture
(This was the first time in the history of the awards that a sequel won Best Picture.)
(2) Best Screenplay Adaptation
(3) Direction
(4) Best Supporting Actor—Robert De Niro
(5) Best Musical Score
(6) Best Art Direction

OSCAR SCORECARD—
THE GODFATHER, PART III (1990)

NOMINATIONS

Best Picture

Best Director—**Francis Coppola**

Best Supporting Actor—**Andy Garcia**

Original Song—**"Promise Me You'll Remember"**

Art Direction

Cinematography

Film Editing

OSCARS WON: NONE

CHAPTER 14

Censorship and The Godfather

IF FRANCIS COPPOLA HAD tried to make *The Godfather* just a few years earlier, it would have been a lamer, tamer film. *The Godfather* was released in 1972. Until 1968 the Code and Rating Administration, popularly known as the Hays Office, wrapped a moral comforter around every film that came out of Hollywood. The Hays Office enforced what has gone down in history as the Hays Code, a set of guidelines that were created by a Catholic priest and a trade journal publisher.

In 1992, hard on the heels of the third *Godfather,* Hollywood finds itself fighting those who would recreate something like the Hays Office and its code. One leader, Cardinal Roger M. Mahoney, has proposed a new decency code for the movies. Dr. Dennis Jarrard, Chairman of Mahoney's Commission on Obscenity and Pornography, has expressed the need for a return to a modified Hays Code, similar to that which existed from the Thirties to the late Sixties.

Other attacks abound. Movie critic Michael Medved has written a highly visible book, *Hollywood Vs America,* in which he lashes out at the abuses of today's moviemakers. And in the 1992 presidential campaign, Vice President Dan Quayle spoke out to condemn the excesses of Hollywood's rulers.

The Ratings System, established by Jack Valenti, former LBJ adviser, is aimed mainly at keeping children out of adult movies. But the religious right today is expressing a longing for the bad old days and the bad old Hays. Between the impulse of some to ban what they consider immoral, and the impulse of others to exploit and pander, free expression often remains an uncomfortable right. But the quality of *The Godfather* and its sequel, which could only have been produced in an atmosphere of free expression, make one fear for the return of censorship that is being promoted today.

Francis Coppola was fortunate that by the time he made *The Godfather* in 1972, the Hays Office and its code had been laid to rest. Among the incidents—and there are many more—that could never have been brought to the screen are:

- Jack Woltz finds a bloody horse's head in his bed.

- Sonny Corleone commits adultery during his sister's wedding.

- Sonny's wife gestures to indicate the prodigious size of her husband's genitals.

- Sonny is machine-gunned to death at a highway tollbooth.

- Barzini refers to the Congressmen that Don Corleone carries in his pocket as "small change."

- Sonny brutalizes his brother-in-law Carlo.

- On her wedding night, Michael's Sicilian bride bares her breasts.

- Jack Woltz calls Italian Americans "guinies," "wops," and "goombahs."

Hollywood hired Will Hays in the Thirties to establish a censorship code to keep films free of sex and violence. Thankfully it had been abandoned by the time *The Godfather* was produced.

- A mobster is garroted, after a knife has been driven through his hand.

- A series of assassinations climax the film.

- Kay tells Michael that she has aborted their child.

- The Don tells Tom Hagen to assign a task to a "Jew Congressman."

- A series of murders intercut with a sacred ceremony.

- The preponderance of Italian names would not have been permitted, since the Hays Code prohibited anything implicitly insulting to an ethnic group.

When reviewing some of the excesses of the censors, one can see how *The Godfather* would have been gutted and its essence drained away. Here is a sampling of the offenses that the censors "cleaned up" before the demise of the Hays Office:

BLASPHEMY:
In *Life With Father,* the famous last line was eliminated as blasphemous.

On his way to church, Father Day says, "I'm going to be baptized, dammit."

NUDITY:
In *The Ten Commandments,* the censors said that "Care is needed in showing Adam and Eve with regard to nudity." In *Spartacus,* there was an injunction that "The loincloth costumes must be adequate."

VULGARITY:
Sometimes the censors' demands went beyond human powers. In *Monkey Business,* the censors said,

The censors trimmed numerous suggestive lines from Marx Brothers movies that seem tame today and have been restored for television.

"Care should be exercised in the scene in which Harpo wrestles with the dowager, to keep it free of vulgarity."

SUGGESTIVE LINES:
The excised lines drifted like petals to the studio floor. In *Pal Joey*, they killed the line "Two years, Vera, that's a long time between drinks." In *A Night at the Opera*, they killed "Lichee nuts to you." In *Notorious*, they deleted "Once aboard the lugger, the girl is mine!" In *The Maltese Falcon*, they objected to Sydney Greenstreet's repeated interjection "By gad!"

PROFANITY:
In *Guys and Dolls*, the censors told the producers to bear in mind that the expression "Hallelujah" was important to many people, and that using "The Star Spangled Banner" to stop a fight was in bad taste. In *Gone With the Wind*, the censors' fought Rhett's final line, "Frankly, my dear, I don't give a damn," and suggested that the thought could be well expressed in other ways, like: "Frankly,

my dear, it's a matter of indifference to me."

POLITICS:
Fearing federal censorship, the movie censors didn't like political leaders to be insulted. Concerning *Mr. Smith Goes to Washington,* the censors wrote, "We suggest you consider the advisability of the line 'You can *buy* the men to come here and get dams legislated.'" The film, said the censors, should emphasize that "Senators and congressmen are sturdy men of integrity."

OBSCENITY:
In Vittorio De Sica's classic *The Bicycle Thief,* they insisted on cutting the scene in which the thief's small son relieves himself and then races through a brothel.

LIBIDINOUS SEX:
In *The Best Years of Our Lives,* the censors reminded the producers, "There should be no open-mouthed kissing." In addition, kisses had a strict time limit. They could not be prolonged. A five-second kiss was romantic, but a six-second kiss was obscene.

DRUG ADDICTION:
Otto Preminger's *Man With the Golden Arm* was made over the express disapproval of the Hays Office and the Catholic Legion of Decency. Similarly, references to narcotics in the meeting of the *Godfather*'s Five Families would have been banned.

Censors tried to remove the line "Frankly, my dear, I don't give a damn" from *Gone With the Wind,* substituting a similar line such as "Frankly, my dear, I don't care."

The censorship code forbid any reference to drugs. Otto Preminger's *The Man with the Golden Arm* challenged the waning power of the Hays Office.

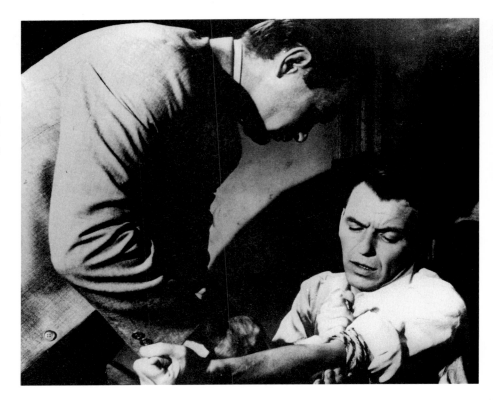

The Godfather was certainly not a movie laden with sex, and the censors were most preoccupied by sex. But they were also concerned with blasphemy and violence, and, as the most violent film in memory, *The Godfather* would certainly have raised their hackles. And *Godfather, Part III* would have been doomed by its reference to corruption in the church. Many found *The Godfather* a brutal and sadistic movie, but most observers fear that a new Hays Office, such as Cardinal Mahoney favors, would see the egregious censorship code rising Phoenix-like from the ashes of today's freedoms.

Today's Ratings Code is certainly not a clear triumph of freedom over repression. Self-censorship still occurs when directors cut their films to assure an "R" rather than an "X" or a "PG" rather than an "R" rating. Whether the voluntary self-policing system under which Francis Coppola created *The Godfather* is still necessary is an ongoing question. Those who defend the system as a prudent way to protect the young, which is its chief reason for being, have a valid concern. The power of the screen is such that to strip away even the modest signposts of the rating system might have its dangers.

Yet *The Godfather* offers an interesting point on the folly of censorship. The end of *Godfather II* shows Michael Corleone stripped of all that has real worth—his wife, his children, his brother, his friendships, his principles, his humanity. He has been stripped of everything but his power. This seems a more fitting and dire penalty than the fatal physical punishment the Hays Office used to require for its Little Caesars and Scarfaces.

CHAPTER 15

Violence on the Screen

THE AMERICAN COLLEGE Dictionary defines *violence* as: rough force in action; injurious treatment; unjust or unwarranted exertion of power; outrage; fury; intensity; severity.

When *The Godfather* first appeared it stirred a fury of objections, an outrage, an intense and severe feeling among critics and audiences concerning all the violence on the screen. People said they couldn't remember a film in which there was such an abundance of violence. But it seemed to many that these critics protested too much. Since sex had been forbidden on the movie

screen by the censors from 1935 to 1968, filmmakers had often fallen back on the "V" word.

At least, when Francis Coppola resorted to violence, and admittedly he did so with some frequency, he did it with a certain panache. No one was simply gunned down. There was always a certain flair to the execution. The victim was trapped in a revolving door. Or shot down by a policeman as he gave a parking ticket. Or shot in the eye on a massage table. Or garroted from the back seat of a car. Or gunned down after buying some pastries.

("Leave the gun, take the cannoles.")

Oscar Levant used to say, "I can stand anything but pain," but for moviegoers, the perception of another's pain is not unpleasant. As a reminder to those who found an excess of violence in *The Godfather,* here is a gallery of violence to remind the reader of the brutality that has pervaded our movies—without the flair and invention that Francis Coppola brought to the business. Here are some of the tools and techniques with which moviemakers have brought violence to the screen:

WEAPONS

1. A flambeau: *Ben Hur*

2. The lash: *The Prodigal*

3. The baling hook: *Santiago*

4. The guillotine: *The Pit and the Pendulum*

5. The spear: *The Prodigal*

6. The revolver: *West Side Story*

7. The pistol: *The Klansman*

8. The hunting knife: *Saskatchewan*

9. The dagger: *The Loves of Omar Khayyam*

10. The stake: *Joan of Arc*

11. The arrow: *The Egyptian*

12. The laser beam: *Goldfinger*

OTHER TYPES OF VIOLENCE

1. Kung Fu: *Return of the Dragon*

2. Fists: *Rocky*

3. Rape: *Demetrius and the Gladiators*

4. Jujitsu: *Moonraker*

5. Pummeling: *Scarlet Angel*

6. Kicking: *Salome*

7. Crushing: *Quo Vadis*

Charleton Heston wields a flambeau in *Ben Hur*.

An infidel feels the sting of the lash in *The Prodigal*.

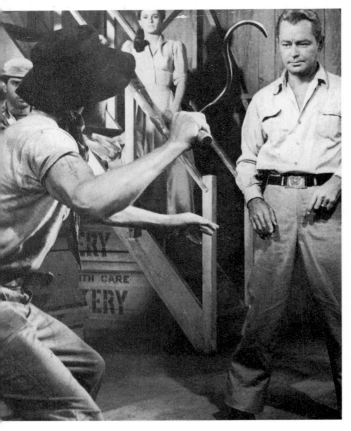

Vincent Price pauses to reflect in *The Pit and the Pendulum*.

Alan Ladd prepares for a baling hook attack in *Santiago*.

A Roman feels a spear's point in *The Prodigal*.

A vengeful Natalie Wood aims a revolver in *West Side Story*.

Lee Marvin levels a .45 caliber pistol at O.J. Simpson in *The Klansman*.

Alan Ladd and Anthony Caruso at knife point in *Saskatchewan*.

An Arabian assault in *The Loves of Omar Khayyam*.

An arrow protrudes from a maiden's breast in *The Egyptian*.

A laser beam approaches James Bond's loafers in *Goldfinger*.

Ingrid Bergman prepares to suffer at the stake in *Joan of Arc*.

Bruce Lee's feet are lethal weapons in *Return of the Dragon*.

Stephan Boyd threatens a maid with a fate worse than death in *Demetrius and the Gladiator*.

Rocky beats off challenger Clubber Lang in *Rocky III*.

Yvonne De Carlo pummels a dancehall girl in *Scarlet Angel*.

Charles Laughton kicks an unworthy pilgrim in *Salome*.

Gladiators entertain upscale Romans in *Quo Vadis*.

CHAPTER 16

The Glorious Sequel

THERE HAVE BEEN fourteen James Bond movies, five Pink Panthers and five Rockies. Sequels generally get made for one basic reason: they give a picture a ready-made momentum because the audience is already sold on the subject. So it was with the *Godfather* sequels. They carried a tremendous inbred appeal.

But a funny thing happened on the way to the sequel. Something quite extraordinary, in fact. Like the original *Godfather* film, *Part II* actually won the Oscar for Best Picture. For both the original and the sequel to win Best Picture Oscars was a *tour de force* unrivaled in movie history. And this occurred in an age when movie sequels are as common as popcorn. When *Godfather, Part II* exploded on the screen it mesmerized

audiences and critics alike, equaling the verve and strength of its distinguished predecessor.

———

Let's admit it. In the entertainment business, "sequel" is a four-letter word. It usually defines a film that was hastily shot (remember the sequel to *The Exorcist?* the sequel to *Poltergeist?*) to exploit the box office profits of its progenitor. Consider the sequels to *Psycho, Lethal Weapon, Friday the 13th, Halloween, Home Alone, Police Academy, Love Story,* and on and on. Studio vaults overflow with the remains of defective "Return tos" and studio executives cringe when plans for sequels are discussed at development meetings.

But the *Godfather* sequel was, from the beginning, "a film of respect," not a cynical exploitation flick. It was one of the most publicized sequels in Hollywood history. It premiered two years after the original *Godfather* began its march to the top of box-office successes. Suddenly the word "sequel" sounded

(ABOVE) Peter Sellers made a flock of sequels to Blake Edwards' *Pink Panther,* about the bumbling police inspector.

(LEFT) Sylvester Stallone made numerous sequels, all of them successful, to *Rocky,* the film about the Philadelphia boxer.

(LEFT) The sequel to Stephen Spielberg's *Poltergeist* somehow lacked the terror of the original.

(BELOW LEFT) There were many canine incarnations in the *Lassie* series.

(BELOW) Marlon Brando helped launch the original *Superman* film, but its sequels have been of declining interest.

respectable. It no longer conjured up thoughts of *Tarzan's New York Adventure* and *Shadow of The Thin Man.* Incredibly, *Godfather II* was unquestionably equal to— and in many ways better than —its lauded forebear.

Conventional wisdom asserts that a sequel is never as good as its predecessor. Conventional wisdom was proved wrong by *Godfather*

II. Many expressed the blasphemous view that it was better than the original. The two-volume video set had a wide sale, and the three-volume video set promises to become a great American film document.

Part II is an exquisitely made, thrilling movie. Not since Bing Crosby brought Father O'Malley back to the screen in *The Bells of St. Mary's,* after his original triumph in *Going My Way,*

had a revisit been so eagerly anticipated.

Francis Coppola had no fondness for sequels. He was disinclined to return to the scene of the crime—sequels bring odious comparisons. It took long months to persuade the director to undertake *Godfather, Part II.*

Finally, Paramount's Peter Bart sat down with the director.

There were numerous sequels to the *Tarzan* film that starred Johnny Weismuller as the original Ape Man.

of young Vito in Sicily. These scenes were part of Puzo's novel and had been intended for inclusion in the first *Godfather* film, but were dropped at the eleventh hour.

Some acts are hard to follow: Sinatra in a nightclub; Moby Dick in a novel; *The Godfather* in a film. The treasury of mobsters, the rich Mafia traditions, the marriage of pop appeal and superior filmmaking made an unbeatable movie.

Coppola had to repeat his success without the inimitable Marlon Brando and the incendiary James Caan. He took a daring step: the sequel became a manifesto. It was a statement on the degrading of the American dream. It was a declaration on the corrupting influence of power. And it worked.

"Francis," he said, "you were the real star of *The Godfather*. What does a star get?"

"A million dollars," said Coppola, citing the figure that super stars traditionally received at that time."

"If I can get you a million dollars to write and direct," said Bart, "will you do it?"

"Yes," said Coppola.

Peter Bart called board chairman Charles Bluhdorn, and told him of his conversation with Coppola. Bluhdorn began to shout.

"Close the deal! Where are the papers! Do it! Do it!"

Eventually, the studio proffered the director complete creative control of *Godfather II*. The million dollars would cover writing, directing, and producing; and there would be a percentage of the gross, as opposed to the more ephemeral net of

the original film. When Coppola agreed, he insisted that the film not be a sequel, but an embellishment of the original.

Thus, whatever the ads and critics say, *Godfather II* is not really a sequel at all. Better to label it an enlargement, an expansion, an elaboration, a "prequel" perhaps—a consideration of what produced this singular family. Viewed together, as they were when they were brought to television, the first two *Godfathers* formed a giant saga. Its last half pictured the corrosion of a family that had shone in its first half: truly a rise and fall of the Corleones.

Coppola set out to make a companion piece. He wanted to use that hoary device, the flashback, to portray the life

After the triumphal success of the original *Godfather*, Coppola took stock. He was not only an artistic visionary, he was a very pragmatic businessman. Coppola admitted:

I could make five failures, five pictures that nobody liked, and I'd still be the only guy who directed The Godfather. *There was only one way to undo that fast, and that was to attempt to make another* Godfather *and fail.* Godfather, Part II *was the riskiest thing I could do. If it bombed, then people would look at the first* Godfather *and say it was all Brando. . . . If I took my career to an insurance actuary, he'd have told me to lay off the sequels if I wanted to stay healthy.*

———

At first, Francis Coppola had no intention of making a sequel to *The Godfather*. But they made him an offer he couldn't refuse. Put in the bluntest of terms, he agreed to do it if he could destroy the Corleone family.

Paramount wasn't pleased with this overall concept. Since the days of Louis B. Mayer and Darryl Zanuck, moviemakers have known that audiences want characters they can root for. Despite what they did, audiences rooted for the Corleones in *Part I*. Said Coppola, "I wanted to put a stop to all that." He was sensitive to the criticism that

For half a century, movie producers have been wary of creating a sequel to *Gone With the Wind,* fearing odious comparisons.

he had validated and glorified the Mafia in the original.

———

The same critics who attacked Coppola for sanitizing gangsters in the original, praised their deflowering in *Part II*. Michael's idealistic instincts become corrupted into ugly and brutish campaigns. While, in the original, Coppola lionized and deified the mobster, in the sequel the family moves into the corrosive arena of political

conflict, and the conscience behind Michael's Ivy League wardrobe has vanished. If director Coppola was enthralled by the power and purpose of these mobsters in *Part I,* he later shows nothing but loathing.

"We will tolerate no guerrillas in the casinos or the swimming pool," says Batista, mocking the threat posed by the surrogate Castro, the rebel who is in the hills. In pre-Castro Havana, we see a wretched Michael—duplicitous, lethal, Machiavellian—very much at home among a gallery of sleazy senators, businessmen, and government officials. Batista's downfall signals the ultimate downfall of Michael's evil empire. In *Godfather I,* Michael, fresh from Dartmouth and a war hero, is pulled inexorably into the family business. But by the end of *Part II,* all of Michael's humane instincts have deserted him.

In *Part I,* there was a whiff of conscience to the Corleone clan. They would not deal in drugs; they would not betray others. But in *Part II* there is the aroma of deceit, double-dealing, and double-crossing. Now, the Corleones seem to be as bereft of morality, as vile and degenerate, as their adversaries.

The director's attitude toward the Mafia has become rigidly pessimistic. There is no more glorification. Just a chilling picture of depraved, amoral behavior.

■

Part II begins in a manner analogous to the original. There is a tight close-up of Michael, the new Godfather, doling out benefactions just as his father had done to the baker and the undertaker. But we perceive that the status of the new don is abrading and wearing down.

He will have his hands full if he is to maintain his position in the teeth of formidable foes: a crooked politician, a Meyer Lansky surrogate, and the majesty of the U.S. Senate. In addition, the young don's wife is importuning him to legitimize the family's interests.

The opening scene dares to emulate the magnificent wedding scene that launched the first film. This time the occasion for the fête is a party for Michael's son, whose operatic debut will climax the third film. The setting is Lake Tahoe, a new Corleone compound from which Michael rules his Las Vegas resources. An unctuous U.S. Senator accepts Michael's contribution to the state university, disdaining his shiny suit and mis-pronouncing his name, as a boys' choir sings a song dedicated to Michael. It is an unwittingly ironic choice: "Mr. Wonderful."

■

All through *Part II*'s three-and-a-half-hour running time, the movie flows back and forth between Little Italy of the early century and Nevada of the Fifties. Ike was in the White House, Elvis was in Graceland, and Joe McCarthy was in his

glory. The scenes of New York in the century's teen years are as evocative as those in the films *Ragtime* and *Once Upon a Time in America.* We see a vendetta played out in the harsh hills of Sicily. And we see the plastic glories of Las Vegas, Miami Beach, and Havana.

■

Paramount was nervous about the ending of the film. It was so grim, so solemn, so downbeat: Michael has his older brother killed. But Paramount had little option, their agreement with Coppola granted him complete creative control. Lacking creative control, the director would have passed on the project. He was not, after all, a masochist, and he felt he had earned the right to call the shots.

Responding to Paramount's concerns, Coppola pondered a marginally more upbeat ending: Michael's son would turn on his father and, in an outburst of acrimony, refuse to assume his place in the family business. But ultimately, Coppola abandoned such speculations.

The crucial thing, for Coppola, was that at the end of the film, Michael has become a vicious, pitiless man. His only criterion and consideration is the business. All else can be freely destroyed without a moment's regret: a wife, a friend, a brother, anyone. Coppola considered this a more ghastly and appalling conclusion for an underworld chief than the customary end, where Cagney or Bogart or Robinson is trapped on a street corner or on the church steps by the men in blue.

___

The power and money that *Godfather II* brought Coppola was accompanied by what Coppola called "the bitch handmaiden of Fame." After *Part II,* Coppola was even more caught up in the life of a celebrity. *Newsweek* did a major story on him; so did *Time;* so did *New York* magazine.

"Who needs it?" snapped Coppola. "Most of the stories . . . make you look like a schmuck and get people mad at you. And then people read about you and decide that you're a millionaire and kidnap your children. And people send you scripts—what do I want to read scripts for? I *write* scripts. It's just not worth it."

CHAPTER 17

Casting the Sequel

T HE CASTING OF *GODFATHER II* did not have the dynamics or disputes of *Godfather I,* because many members of the cast were already in place and had established their roles in the original. Ironically, this made the cast additions especially important: the newcomers had to bring freshness and invigoration.

An obscure actor named Robert De Niro wanted to read for the role of the hotheaded, murderous Sonny Corleone in the original *Godfather.* The director thought he was too slight of build to play the brutish Sonny, who was painted by Puzo as a violent ruffian. Coppola asked De Niro to read for the part of Michael instead. His image of Michael was more diminutive. Eventually Coppola decided on Al Pacino to play Michael Corleone and cast De Niro in the role of Paulie Gato, the Godfather's chauffeur, the Judas who betrays him and facilitates his assassination among the vegetables. ("Paulie called in sick.")

Pacino's selection as Michael set Paramount's attorneys bustling to resolve his prior commitment to MGM: Pacino had signed to appear in another mobster film, *The Gang That Couldn't Shoot Straight,* based on Jimmy Breslin's comic novel about a Mafia mob. De Niro felt he had a chance of getting Pacino's part in the Breslin movie. Recalls Coppola, "Bobby came to me and said he had a problem. He had a definite part from me [the chauffeur] but he had the possibility of the Pacino role in *The Gang That Couldn't Shoot Straight.* He didn't want to give up the one and couldn't honestly go back [to MGM] and try for the other if he was committed elsewhere. . . . So I said I'd hold the role of the chauffeur, in case he didn't get the other part which, as it turned out, he got. But I got something too. I got Bobby in *Part II,* which I couldn't have done if I'd held him to his commitment in *Part I.*"

If Coppola was concerned that another studio had a Mafia film in progress

concurrent with *The Godfather,* he showed no signs of apprehension. While he was writing the *Godfather II* script, another director with a taste for Italian mobsters in film, Martin Scorsese, showed Francis a movie he'd just completed that starred this selfsame Robert De Niro. It was called *Mean Streets* and De Niro played an erratic character named Johnny Boy. "It kept rolling around in my head," said Coppola, "that De Niro's face reminded me of Vito Corleone. . . . The Godfather had the [same] accentuated jaw, the kind of funny smile . . . the strong cheekbones and jowls. De Niro was certainly believable as someone in the Corleone family and quite possibly Pacino's father."

Coppola invited De Niro out to an Italian restaurant (naturally) to refresh his memory and check out the actor's facial geography: could he play a believable young Brando? Life is what goes on while we are making other plans. De Niro had not the foggiest notion that he was being considered for the pivotal role in *Godfather, Part*

In filming De Niro as the young Vito Corleone, the producers first tried to recast his face to more closely resemble Brando, then discarded the idea.

II, the part that would lift his career to a new plateau.

Today, Robert De Niro seems a logical choice. But in 1974 he had not yet established himself in such galvanizing roles as *Raging Bull* and *Taxi Driver.* At the point when Coppola was weighing him as a possible young Vito Corleone, De Niro was an unorthodox actor. He had only played eccentrics and amusing imbeciles (for example, the disturbed Johnny Boy in *Mean Streets* and the sub-literate baseball player in *Bang the Drum Slowly*). Predictably, the studio balked, but Coppola prevailed. Perhaps he had grown confident of his casting acumen after winning the earlier battles on Brando and Pacino.

To capture the Brando look more closely, the makeup people tried first to recast De Niro's face, but this idea was discarded. It is the Actors Studio credo that sheer acting is better than the dissimulations of makeup. (Dustin Hoffman, another Actors Studio alumni, went sleepless for days to prepare himself for a scene in *Marathon Man*. Laurence Olivier smiled wryly and said, "Dear boy, next time try acting.") But De Niro did study film of Brando's performance in *The Godfather* and he tried to emulate his bearing, his manner, and his hoarse voice.

———

Newsmen called him "the Godfather of the Godfathers," "the Chairman of the Board of the National Crime Syndicate," "the Mafia's banker." He was Meyer Lansky, fictionally represented by Hyman Roth in *Godfather II*. But who was to play the role of this embodiment of brains, sophistication, and sheer cleverness in crime? Elia Kazan was the first choice to play the diminutive Jewish underworld chief. Ironically, Kazan was the director who Coppola feared would replace him as director of *Godfather I* when Paramount grew unhappy with the rushes.

When Coppola appeared at Elia Kazan's office, the director of *A Streetcar Named Desire* was shirtless. Coppola was struck by the image of an elderly man sans shirt, and he wrote in a scene where Hyman Roth is shirtless.

Elia Kazan turned down

the role and Coppola wound up with another legendary director, Lee Strasberg. This would be the first time he had ever acted on film. Strasberg, a protean seventy-three, headed the Actors Studio, which had nurtured Marlon Brando and taught him his craft, as it had also trained or influenced an entire generation of actors—Al Pacino, Dustin Hoffman, Robert De Niro, and Eli Wallach—who would be featured in *Godfather III*.

Because Francis Coppola was too diffident to simply phone the fabled Strasberg for a meeting, a mutual friend planned a dinner party so that the two men might "accidentally" meet. Strasberg got the role of Hyman Roth/Meyer Lansky and, to no one's surprise, made of it a personal triumph. Seventeen years later, Ben Kingsley played Meyer Lansky in *Bugsy,* but it is Strasberg's performance that remains with us.

It was Al Pacino, a friend and former member of the Actors Studio, who suggested Lee Strasberg for the role of Hyman Roth. Strasberg is generally believed to have founded the Actors Studio, but actually he was named its Artistic Director by Elia Kazan shortly after its birth. Kazan then opened the door to another Strasberg

opportunity by turning down the role of Hyman Roth.

———

Success in acting is a mixture of talent and assertion. Bruno Kirby could not read for the part of the young Clemenza in *Godfather II* for the simple reason that the part was written in Italian and, though of Italian extraction, he could not speak the language. Bruno's father Bruce Kirby, a fine character actor, had accompanied his son to the audition with Coppola and it is fortunate for Bruno that he did. The director asked Kirby senior if his son spoke Italian. Recalled Bruno, "My father, who is of the 'Say yes' school of acting, said that I did, though I don't speak a word. Francis started to speak to me in Italian, and I couldn't understand anything he said."

"I thought he spoke Italian," said Coppola.

"Street Italian," said Bruce Kirby, "a word here, a word there. Do you have a part for him?"

"I've got lots of parts. Don't worry about it," said Coppola airily.

"It was a terrible interview," recalled Bruno Kirby. "I thought it was all over." But it wasn't.

A few years before, Kirby had been up for a television gang comedy called

When Coppola visited Elia Kazan to offer him the role of Hyman Roth, Kazan was barechested. This gave Coppola the image of a naked torso for Lee Strasberg, who played the role.

"Where's the Fire?" and had told the producers he did not want to be typecast in comedy roles. He wanted, he said, to work in serious films with serious actors "like Robert De Niro."

As everyone in the civilized world knows, Marlon Brando was not in the sequel to *The Godfather.* He was missed, but most audiences and critics could feel his presence. His soul seemed to be suspended over the proceedings like an omnipotent spirit.

The director had badly wanted Brando in one scene of the sequel, the scene that closes the film—the flashback to the birthday party on the day the Japanese attack Pearl Harbor, when Michael announces he has joined the Marines. Brando flatly refused. He was furious with Paramount executive Frank Yablanz who, in turn, was enraged at Brando for turning down the Academy Award.

The character of Clemenza, the man who taught Michael to make a creditable tomato sauce in *Part I,* was written out of the sequel. It seems that Richard Castellano, who played him in the original, was demanding an extravagant salary, plus the privilege of rewriting his own dialogue.

Al Pacino also knew that "sequel" was considered a dirty word, and wasn't particularly anxious to make one. He felt, understandably, that it would be redundant. He had already played an Ivy Leaguer turned gangster. He'd be doing a second carbon. But Pacino, too, received an offer he couldn't refuse. He agreed to make the movie when Coppola assured him that Michael would age to eighty, an irresistible challenge to any actor. The aging did not, in fact, take place. (Pacino was not to be seen in such an antiquated state until the closing moments of *Godfather III.*)

That was not quite the end of the Pacino problem. A week before *Godfather II* was to begin shooting, Al Pacino announced that he didn't much like the scenes in which he appeared. He importuned the director to rewrite them. Just in time for the first rehearsal, Coppola completed the rewrite and Pacino was placated.

In shooting *Part II,* Coppola's movable feast of moviemaking traveled from Lake Tahoe to Santo Domingo (which served as Cuba in the pre-Castro days). The Santo Domingo climate was not hospitable: the company was rained out day after day. It was especially inhospitable for Pacino: he caught pneumonia.

The editing process in moviemaking can be a tangled web. In *Godfather II,* it threatened to become uncontrollable. Major scenes and segments of the film were being changed or dropped. People in the know feared that the film would not meet its opening-day commitments. For a film as eagerly awaited and promoted as *Godfather II,* this was calamitous. Of course, shortly before *Godfather I* opened in triumph, "people in the know" had said it was unreleasable.

The director George S. Kaufman had once said of San Diego, "You don't go there unless you're invited." Paramount was not invited, but two weeks before the world premiere of *Godfather, Part II,* they held a sneak preview in San Diego. Everyone in the studio bureaucracy felt the movie had serious defects: its final hour was disordered, muddled, chilly.

During the preview, the audience seemed adrift in a quagmire of flashbacks and plot contortions. As the film unrolled, Coppola slumped in his seat and mumbled notes into a tape recorder. What scenes weren't playing well? Which ones needed to be lengthened? Which ones needed to be shortened? Which needed to be deleted? Did they really need an Intermission?

Complained Coppola, "I started out to make a film about a man obsessed with his father's success on the eve of his own failure. A story of succession, juxtaposing the father and the son at approximately the same ages; the father in his rise and the son in his fall. And that's hard to do. So for a long time there, I had two films that didn't make sense together. . . . Never never never again will I work under such chaotic conditions," said Coppola.

But the changes were made in time for the premiere and *Godfather, Part II* was greeted by an avalanche of popular and critical approval.

CHAPTER 18

Things Change

SIXTEEN YEARS PASSED between the appearance of *Godfather II* and *Godfather III,* from 1974 to 1990. During that time, Paramount engaged the services of a wide variety of screenwriters, directors, and studio executives to create an idea that was worthy of the rich lineage of the first two films. They had, after all, been the only movies in history to win Best Picture Oscars for a movie and its sequel. They had generated an annuity for Paramount stockholders and their heritage could not be lightly squandered. Finally, they turned to Coppola with still another offer he could not refuse.

While creative ferment was taking place, the world continued to turn for a decade and a half. Things change, as playwright David Mamet and others have observed, and here is a picture of the changes in the world between the year when *Godfather II* reached the screen, and the year when *Godfather III* finally appeared.

Richard Nixon was President.
George Bush was President.

Spiro Agnew was Vice President.
Dan Quayle was Vice President.

Teddy Kennedy was Senator from Massachusetts.
Teddy Kennedy is Senator from Massachusetts.

Dr. Henry Kissinger was Secretary of State.
Dr. Henry Kissinger is under contract to ABC News.

The year of *Godfather II,* Henry Kissinger was Secretary of State. The year of *Godfather III,* he was under contract to ABC News.

The year of *Godfather II,* Ron Zeigler was Presidential press secretary. The year of *Godfather III,* he was the head of lobby of druggists.

Ron Zeigler was Nixon's Press Secretary.

Ron Zeigler is head of a druggists' lobbying group.

Ron Howard premiered in *Happy Days.*

Ron Howard is a movie director.
Happy Days is a favorite daily re-run.

Michael Landon premiered in *Little House on the Prairie.*

Michael Landon dies of cancer.

Top television shows included
All in the Family, The Jeffersons and *Mash.*

All in the Family, The Jeffersons and *Mash*
are seen in rerun.

The top male box office stars included
Steve McQueen, John Wayne, and Burt Reynolds.

Steve McQueen is dead of cancer, John Wayne is dead
of cancer, Burt Reynolds stars in a television show.

The top female box office star was singer
Barbra Streisand.

Barbra Streisand has given up singing for directing.

Peter Benchley published *Jaws,*
the story of a killer shark.

Peter Benchley published *Beast,*
the story of a killer squid.

Nicholas Meyer wrote the bestseller
The Seven-Per-Cent Solution.

Nicholas Meyer writes *Star Trek VI.*

Broadway musicals included *Mack and Mabel* by Jerry Herman and *Over Here!* by the Sherman Brothers.

Broadway musicals are dominated by Andrew Lloyd Webber.

All car sales were down.

American car sales are down.

Al Downing gave Henry Aaron his 715th home run to break Babe Ruth's record.

Al Downing is a radio talk show host in Los Angeles.

Kareem Abdul-Jabbar made the NBA all-pro team.

Kareem Abdul-Jabbar retires.

John Newcombe was a world tennis champion.

John Newcombe does play-by-play from Forest Hills.

The year of *Godfather II*, Nixon and Brezhnev held a summit. The year of *Godfather III*, Bush and Gorbachev exchanged New Year's greetings.

Nixon and Brezhnev held a summit.

Bush and Gorbachev exchange New Year's greetings.

Nixon was ordered to yield tapes on the Watergate scandal.

Reagan was ordered to yield his diaries on Iran-Contra scandal.

The year of *Godfather II*, Richard Nixon had been ordered to yield the Watergate tapes. The year of *Godfather III*, he had just published another book as an elder statesman.

The year of *Godfather II*, Willie Brandt resigned as German Prime Minister. The year of *Godfather III*, Germany had been reunited after 45 years of division.

| Sinatra called women "broads and hookers." |
| Kitty Kelley implies Sinatra had trysts with Nancy Reagan. |

| Democrats held the majority in Congress. |
| Democrats hold the majority in Congress. |

| John Ehrlichman was sentenced for Ellsberg violation. |
| Pete Rose is sentenced for tax evasion. |

| Israel and Egypt signed a troop-disengagement accord. |
| Nine Israelis are slain in a bus raid in Egypt. |

| Willie Brandt resigned as German Prime Minister. |
| Germany unites after forty-five years of division. |

| Nelson Rockefeller was appointed Vice President. |
| The Japanese buy Rockefeller Center. |

The year of *Godfather II*, Gerald Ford was sworn in as President. The year of *Godfather III*, he was a successful speaker on the lecture circuit.

| Nixon resigned and Ford was sworn in as President. |
| Nixon writes a new book and Ford enters a golf tournament. |

| Fidel Castro ruled Cuba. |
| Fidel Castro rules Cuba. |

The year of *Godfather II*, Fidel Castro ruled Cuba. The year of *Godfather III*, Fidel Castro ruled Cuba.

CHAPTER 19

Finding the Story
for Godfather III

THERE HAD BEEN TWELVE Tarzan movies, eighteen Charlie Chans, twenty-two Andy Hardys, five Thin Mans, fourteen James Bonds, five Pink Panthers, four Rockies, three Rambos—but only two Godfathers. *Godfather III* was the film everyone wanted to see but no one could manage to make. The principal impediment was finding a viable script.

Putting together a script for *Godfather III* was a tortuous project. In *Sunday in the Park With George,* Stephen Sondheim describes the art of making art as, "putting it together . . . bit by bit." This is the painful process by which an artist advances, compromises, retreats, survives, declines, and prevails. It is the process that comes to mind as one studies how the script of *Godfather III* developed.

Five years before *Godfather III* was released, and a decade after *Godfather II* had opened, there was feverish activity in Hollywood to bring a third *Godfather* to the screen. Paramount knew there

The central edifice in *Godfather I* was the Corleone compound in New York; in *Godfather II* it was the Lake Tahoe estate; in *Godfather III* it was the Vatican in Rome.

would be tremendous profits in another creditable sequel. With the monumental success of its two predecessors, the movie would be a surefire hit. So they unstintingly plundered their treasury for the funds to develop it and spent about $800,000 commissioning storylines, treatments, and

full screenplays in an effort to "get a handle" on the project. But with a property as valuable as *The Godfather,* caution has to be exercised in creating a sequel. So although anxious to make *Godfather III* flower, Paramount nurtured it with great care.

Here are the chief players

NANCY OHANIAN

Francis Coppola   Charles Bludhorn   John Travolta   Robert Evans   Sylvester Stallone   Nick Marino   Stanley Jaffe   Eddie Murphy   Vincent Patrick   Diane Keaton   Al Ruddy

in the creative drama, the people who were "putting it together":

MICHAEL EISNER

was a former president of Paramount and was now chairman of the "mouse factory," as some called the Disney Studios. Under his stewardship, Paramount had become the "hot" studio in town, and he had gone on to bring energy and earnings to the moribund moviemaking process at Disney. During his Paramount years he had sought ideas for the third *Godfather* project, but never felt confident in those he received. Writers trotted in with tales of Kennedys and Cubans and assassinations, but Eisner remained dissatisfied. He had an excellent story sense (Eisner himself wrote a story for

Godfather III). But each time, the project reached a dead end.

BARRY DILLER

had been Eisner's superior in their days at ABC television. Now, three years after the triumphal opening of *Godfather II,* Barry Diller was Paramount's Chairman of the Board. Diller's superior, Charles Bluhdorn, chairman of Paramount's parent company, wanted another *Godfather* sequel. In deference to Bluhdorn, Diller persevered. He called writer/director Richard Brooks. Brooks had written some riveting novels himself, such as *The Brick Foxhole,* and made successful films from others, including *Looking for Mr. Goodbar* and *In Cold Blood.* Brooks was no stranger to fictionalized

urban terror, due to his work on *Blackboard Jungle*. Diller asked Brooks to fly to Miami to meet with Charles Bluhdorn.

RICHARD BROOKS

was greeted at Miami Airport by Bluhdorn's son Paul and a chauffeur. The director hadn't the foggiest notion of the reason for his odyssey. The limo sped across the tarmac to a waiting corporate jet. Two hours later Brooks stepped onto a runway in the Dominican Republic, where he was greeted by a beaming Charles Bluhdorn and a platoon of infantrymen, each wielding machine guns.

CHARLES BLUHDORN,

the conglomerate chairman, handed Richard Brooks an envelope containing a fifty-page treatment. The director

Michael Eisner Barry Diller Don Simpson Marlon Brando Peter Bart Richard Brooks Frank Mancuso Dawn Steel Mario Puzo Al Pacino

sat poolside, turning the pages, and noticed that Bluhdorn was standing on the balcony of his estate, peering at him through binoculars, trying to perceive how interested he was. Recalled Brooks, "It took me two hours to read the treatment and at the end I knew I didn't want to make it. Bluhdorn was pressing me to continue a story that had already ended." But Brooks told the chairman he would think about it.

There comes a time when you have to vote yea or nay. A week later, back in Los Angeles, Brooks phoned Bluhdorn and told him he did not want to make the film. Bluhdorn was so angry and disappointed, he was speechless. Furious, he handed the receiver to an aide.

DON SIMPSON,

Paramount's head of production, who had such films as *Top Gun* in his future, received an interoffice memo from his superior, Michael Eisner. It outlined a possible story for *Godfather III*. The CIA and the Mafia join forces to murder a Latin-American dictator. (There had been rumors of a CIA-Mafia joint venture to assassinate Castro.) In the story, a G-man and a Mafia chief are plunged into each other's world, their characters are exchanged, and ultimately they kill one another. (If this story taxes credibility, it is no more baroque than the theory later spun by Oliver Stone in *JFK*.) The tale found few adherents and was abandoned.

MARIO PUZO

seemed the logical person to write *Godfather III*. After all, he had started the whole business. So in June 1978, Charles Bluhdorn directed Barry Diller to sign Puzo immediately to write a treatment, based on an idea of Bluhdorn's. But by now Mario Puzo had donned his novelist's hat and was writing a new book called *The Sicilian*. He did not wish to return to the *Godfather* wars. Once again, they made him an offer he couldn't refuse. Puzo was given $250,000 for a fifty-page treatment, plus six percent of the gross. This was one of the most lucrative writing deals in history.

Like Richard Brooks, Puzo made a pilgrimage to the Dominican Republic, where Bluhdorn told him his

In one proposed story, the Mafia and the CIA join forces to kill a Latin American dictator. There had been rumors that the CIA had enlisted the aid of the Mafia to kill Castro.

story idea. It was a well-developed storyline and the chairman recounted it at length. Puzo told his attorney, "If I can just get him to write it out . . . I'll just change a few words and turn it back in again with my name on it."

The Puzo-Bluhdorn story focuses on Michael's son Anthony, beginning with his graduation from Annapolis. Anthony and Michael are alienated. Michael is suffering from mental illness and living a sequestered life near Lake Tahoe. The CIA recruits Anthony to kill a South-American dictator.

When the Corleone family learns of Anthony's assignment, it extracts a promise from the government: a corrupt union boss must be freed from federal prison. The Corleone

family trades this favor for some borrowed money from the union pension fund. The Corleones need the cash to bankroll a new casino in Atlantic City. Then a Senate committee investigates CIA involvement in the assassination and, fearing exposure, the CIA decides that Anthony must be terminated. A CIA hit man bungles the job and Anthony lives. He moves in with his father, takes over the Corleone operations, and becomes the new Godfather. Fade to black, slow but final.

JOHN TRAVOLTA,
star of *Grease* and *Saturday Night Fever,* was under consideration by Paramount to play the role of Anthony Corleone. Ronald Reagan was supposed to have the role played by Paul Henreid

in *Casablanca.* If you can picture Reagan on the runway with Bogart and Bergman, then perhaps you can imagine John Travolta as Anthony Corleone.

ROBERT EVANS
had been head of worldwide production at Paramount when the first *Godfather* appeared; in the Eighties he was an independent producer on the Paramount lot. In the space of a few years, *Godfather I* and *II* had become instant classics—*Citizen Kanes* of the Seventies. They were the first of the blockbusters and had flooded Paramount with profits and prestige. His view was, "Of course Paramount should make *III*. There is an audience out there that wants to see it and that's what the movie business is about."

SYLVESTER STALLONE
was involved in one deal whereby he would star in and direct *Godfather III.* It was felt, given his ability to create a commercial and appealing story in the *Rocky* films, Stallone might shepherd *III* safely into port. If you can imagine John Travolta as the Godfather's son, you will have no trouble picturing Sly Stallone as both the new Godfather and the creator of the new story. The studio was trying to protect the value of the

Godfather name by enlisting the most viable stars. But the deal was never consummated.

NICK MARINO

was a street-smart New York movie theater owner who claimed having a relative in the underworld would lend his work verisimilitude. He collaborated on a script for *Part III* with Thomas Lee Wright, an ex-Paramount production executive. Their screenplay, titled *The Family Continues,* took eight months to write and became the seventh try at a workable story for *Godfather III.* Marino was optimistic. He told the press, "We've got [it]. The other people who tried just missed the boat." But apparently the boat sailed without Marino and Wright. Four days after they submitted their scenario, they were notified that Paramount had passed.

In the Marino-Wright opus, Michael and the family had spread to Atlantic City. But the Corleones become endangered by Irish gangsters who threaten to denounce them to the FBI. Anthony has just graduated from college and has learned his street smarts from Sonny's son, Vincent. Tom Hagen and Vincent are murdered, and the Judas of the family, we learn, is sister Connie. She slaughters Michael. (She is still bitter about the death

of her husband Carlo.) Anthony becomes the new Godfather.

ALEXANDER JACOBS

had co-authored the screenplay for the crime classic, *The French Connection.* Jacobs took a crack at a screenplay for *Part III.* In his conception, Michael dies of cancer and Anthony takes on the crown of power. He heads an insurance and investment firm and wants to make the Corleone family's business entirely lawful. But Anthony's cousin undermines the plan for legitimacy. Tom Hagen is murdered and so is the cousin, and Anthony survives to control the family's interests.

DEAN REISNER

again demonstrated how often these failed screenplays tied underworld violence to political violence. In the late Seventies, Dean Reisner, one of the most esteemed writers of crime fiction in Hollywood, submitted a treatment for *Godfather III* that linked the Corleone family and the CIA in the murder of a foreign dictator. In this version, Michael is again living a reclusive life in Tahoe. His son Anthony is in Vietnam, where he acts heroically, is wounded, and returns to the States. He takes up life on a houseboat in Georgetown, Washington, D.C.

A deal was developed whereby Sylvester Stallone would direct and star in *Godfather III,* but it was never consummated.

Tom Hagen finds Anthony and suggests that he visit his father. Michael tells Anthony that the family's welfare is menaced by a rival mob. During Anthony's visit, a bomb explodes and triggers a war between the families. Meanwhile, the Government pursues Anthony, who is implicated in the assassination of a Latin tyrant. To clear the stage of threats to the Corleone family, Anthony must perform the twin prodigies of disposing of the

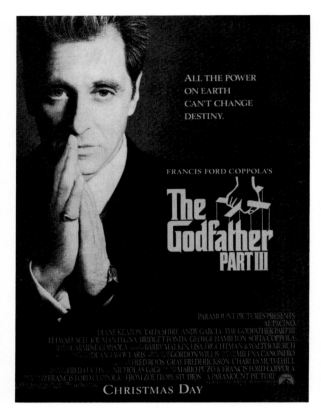

All the power on earth can't change destiny.

FRANCIS FORD COPPOLA'S

The Godfather Part III

PARAMOUNT PICTURES PRESENTS
AL PACINO
DIANE KEATON TALIA SHIRE ANDY GARCIA THE GODFATHER PART III
ELI WALLACH JOE MANTEGNA BRIDGET FONDA GEORGE HAMILTON SOFIA COPPOLA
CARMINE COPPOLA "BARRY MALKIN, LISA FRUCHTMAN & WALTER MURCH
DEAN TAVOULARIS "GORDON WILLIS "MILENA CANONERO
FRED ROOS GRAY FREDERICKSON CHARLES MULVEHILL
FRED FUCHS "NICHOLAS GAGE "MARIO PUZO & FRANCIS FORD COPPOLA
FRANCIS FORD COPPOLA FROM ZOETROPE STUDIOS A PARAMOUNT PICTURE

CHRISTMAS DAY

An ad announces the Christmas pre-miere of *Godfather III.* Paramount felt a Christmas opening was best. They had opened *Part II* at Christ-mas and targeted the original for Christmas.

CIA men and the other Mafia family.

Reisner, whose judgment in these matters is well respected, reflects that the script was injured by the committee's control of the script-writing process. "I've always had the most luck," he says, "with the scripts the studios do the least fiddling with. . . . When you start putting it through the hopper and everyone has their say, it becomes like a smooth ball bearing."

(PREVIOUS PAGES) Ultimately Coppola directed *Godfather III,* whose cast in-cluded Joe Mantegna, Eli Wallach, Andy Garcia, and Al Pacino.

VINCENT PATRICK
was paid $75,000 to write a treatment for *Godfather III* in the early Eighties. This addition to the groaning shelf of *Godfather* creations opened with a bang: the murder of Michael Corleone and Tom Hagen when a car blows up, before the Main Titles roll. Sonny Corleone's son, Santino, takes over the family's affairs, but they clearly require someone with better credentials. So the Corleones recruit Gaetano, Vito Corleone's illegitimate son. He had been dispatched to Sicily as a child and has gained power there. Gaetano is an authoritative fellow who could eat Santino alive. He orders a clutch of killings that trigger a full-scale war between the underworld families.

This time, Anthony is a student at Harvard. The feds use Anthony to rescue a NATO official who has been abducted by Italian terrorists. Then Santino too is kidnapped by a Cuban gang operating in New York. After Santino's rescue, Gaetano tries to have both him and Anthony killed, but fails. These failed assassinations, as we have seen, can be fatal to the perpetrator. Santino and Anthony concoct a grisly end for Gaetano: a priest strangles him with the belt from his robes. Vincent Patrick's story found little favor and joined the others on the shelf of the Story Department.

THE SYMPATHETIC KILLERS:
Note that a common thread uniting many of these misfired scripts is the mantle of power passed from Michael to his son. Also, none of the new screenplays lacked for brutality or foreign intrigue. The chief shortcoming, according to studio decision makers, was the shortage of sympathetic people. "The problem," lamented one studio memo, "is the lack of real or likable characters." Said another, "The focus has been on plotting rather than characterization."

The principals in the first two *Godfather* films were both evil and likable, appalling and appealing. If they murdered with ease and barbarity, they seemed to act only in their justified self-interest. The Corleones were not wanton slaughterers. They were serious men defending their own welfare.

REENTER COPPOLA AND PUZO:
So the search for a plausible storyline continued. But

there was a money problem along with the creative one. Thanks to their success in *The Godfather,* the actors who had been hired for $35,000 to appear in the original *Godfather*—Pacino, Caan, Duvall—now commanded huge salaries. Who could afford to reassemble them?

But, first came the words. Paramount finally turned to the writers of *Godfather I* and *II* to write the third film in the saga.

Coppola had been insistent in declaring his antipathy, aversion, and distaste toward creating a third part of the *Godfather* legend. "I should only have as much money as Francis doesn't want to do another *Godfather,*" said one Paramount wag. Who can fully understand the chemistry and commitment that move the creative spirit? Suffice it to say, in the summer of 1989, Paramount Pictures proposed to give Coppola absolute freedom in the development of the third part of the saga. The terms would be entirely his, and he would not be tied to any of the abortive scripts and storylines that the studio had created. And so, Coppola seized the cup. If Gall is divided into three parts, so too would be the *Godfather* saga.

By now time was growing

short: Francis Coppola was given only six weeks to write the screenplay. He had asked for six months. Coppola and Puzo sequestered themselves in Reno for three days in 1989 to sketch an outline for the story. Coppola came up with the first half of the film —Puzo the second half. Then the halves were "nailed together." During the eight months that followed, the duo rewrote no less than twelve drafts of *Godfather III.* In November 1989 shooting began. The director had set late 1991 as his target for completion of the film, but Paramount had other ideas. It wanted to release the film for Christmas 1990. There was precedent: *Godfather II* had a Christmas opening and a Christmas premiere had been planned for *Godfather I* as well. The marketing men felt the holidays were the best time for a *Godfather* release. Have yourself a sanguinary Christmas. . . .

For those who have seen *Godfather III,* which must be virtually everyone, it is interesting to note that Coppola and Puzo considered no less than five possible endings for the film:

1. Michael dies of diabetes.
2. Mary is killed by mistake. Michael dies of old age.
3. Michael survives, blinded, to contemplate his sins.

When Robert Duvall's financial demands could not be met, the new consiglieri was played by George Hamilton.

Eddie Murphy called Coppola and Puzo and expressed a serious interest in a role in *Godfather III.*

4. Michael is assassinated and dies in Vincent's arms.
5. Michael commits suicide by seizing a mobster's gun and blowing his own brains out on the steps of the opera house.

CHAPTER 20

The Corleone Family Trees

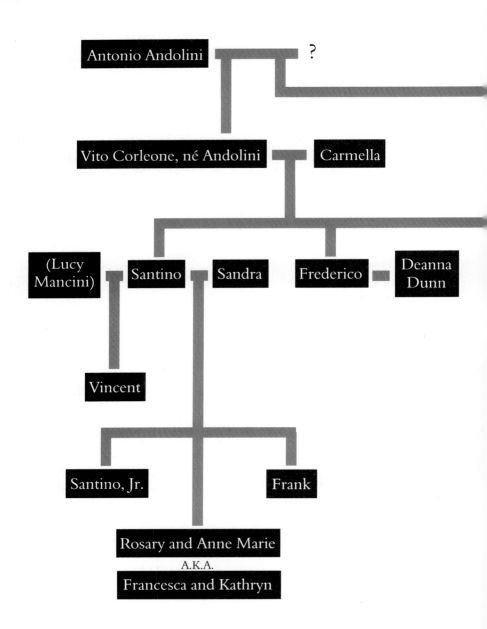

Antonio Andolini _____ ?

Vito Corleone, né Andolini _____ Carmella

(Lucy Mancini) — Santino — Sandra — Frederico — Deanna Dunn

Vincent

Santino, Jr. _____ Frank

Rosary and Anne Marie
A.K.A.
Francesca and Kathryn

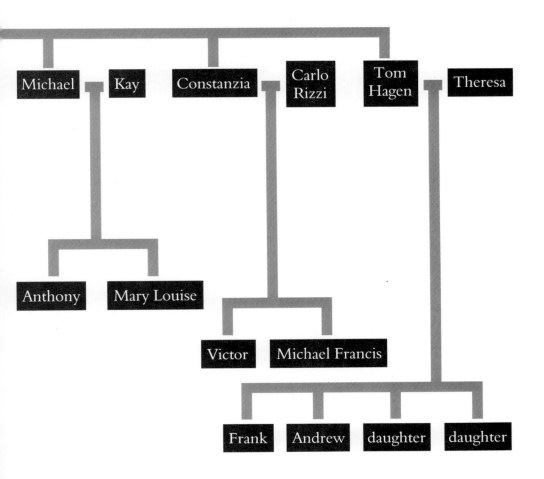

Paolo Andolini

Michael   Kay   Constanzia   Carlo Rizzi   Tom Hagen   Theresa

Anthony   Mary Louise

Victor   Michael Francis

Frank   Andrew   daughter   daughter

THE CORLEONE CRIME FAMILY

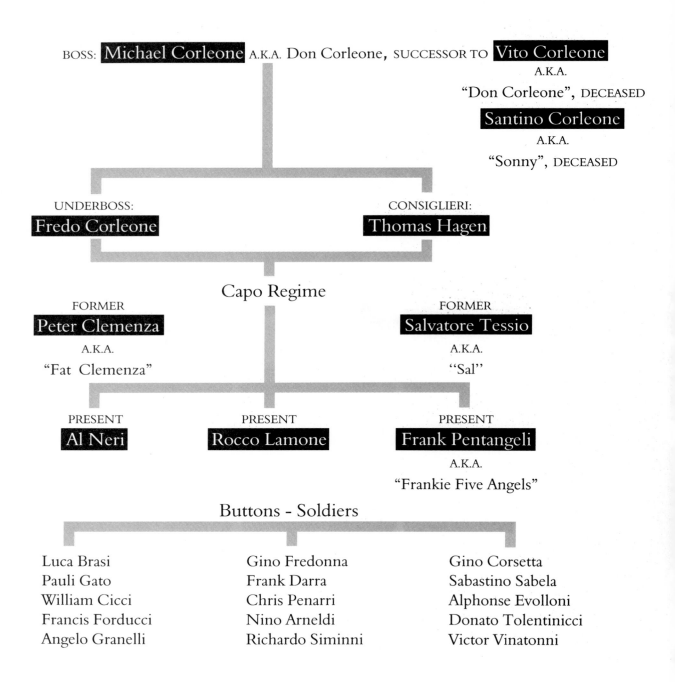

BOSS: Michael Corleone A.K.A. Don Corleone, SUCCESSOR TO Vito Corleone

A.K.A.

"Don Corleone", DECEASED

Santino Corleone

A.K.A.

"Sonny", DECEASED

UNDERBOSS:
Fredo Corleone

CONSIGLIERI:
Thomas Hagen

Capo Regime

FORMER
Peter Clemenza

A.K.A.

"Fat Clemenza"

FORMER
Salvatore Tessio

A.K.A.

"Sal"

PRESENT
Al Neri

PRESENT
Rocco Lamone

PRESENT
Frank Pentangeli

A.K.A.

"Frankie Five Angels"

Buttons - Soldiers

Luca Brasi	Gino Fredonna	Gino Corsetta
Pauli Gato	Frank Darra	Sabastino Sabela
William Cicci	Chris Penarri	Alphonse Evolloni
Francis Forducci	Nino Arneldi	Donato Tolentinicci
Angelo Granelli	Richardo Siminni	Victor Vinatonni

CHAPTER 21

Press Frenzy Greets Godfather III

I T HAD BEEN 16 YEARS SINCE the last *Godfather* epic. Paramount had fifty million dollars riding on the film. For Coppola, the stakes were even higher. Amid endless rewrites, on-set dramas, and spiraling budgets, Coppola was under the gun again. His film must prove his vision, perhaps produce another masterpiece. In the darkness before the Don, the press went wild.

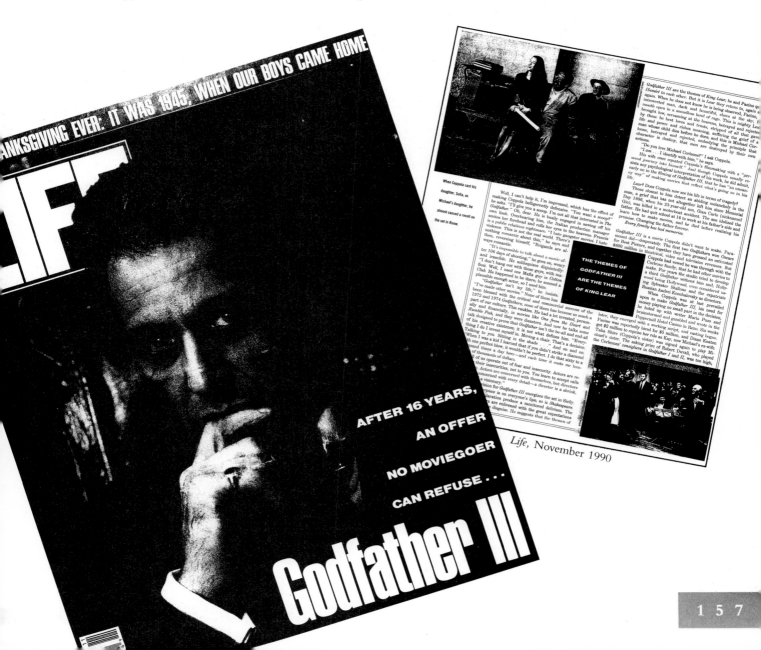

Life, November 1990

the godfather diary

The *Godfather* saga is in many ways also the Coppola family saga. Eleanor Coppola, whose entire family has been involved in the three productions, kept a diary throughout. Here, excerpts from her personal journals on the making of *The Godfather Part III*

October 8, 1989. On an Airplane

I am flying with Francis on the first leg of our journey to location for *The Godfather Part III*. I feel emotions moving along old paths. Yesterday I hugged Roman (our son) goodbye as we left for the airport. I can still feel his thick hair in my hand as my arms were around his neck. I won't see him until Christmas.

When we arrived at our house in L.A., Fred (Fred Roos, a producer and casting director) was waiting on the front porch with a box of videotapes. We settled into the living room and I watched as they went through the casting process, picking actors for parts, eliminating others. I thought how each person would feel when they got the news. I fell asleep on the couch suddenly exhausted from the last weeks, with cast rehearsals at Napa and preparations to leave home for five months.

October 20, 1989. Rome

When we arrived at Fumicino Airport (Rome) a VIP car and escort met us on the tarmac and took us to the terminal ahead of all the other passengers. Our escort said, with excitement and a heavy accent, "Welcome to *Roma*. You are the director of the film *Stepfather*." When the young woman took our passports and read Francis's name, she called to the girl in the next booth and they giggled excitedly.

October 21, 1989. Rome

I am in a second-floor office at Cinecittà, the Italian film studio. New offices have been prepared for Francis's production here in the space that used to be Fellini's. I can hear Francis's voice loud and urgent as he conducts a script conference. The script is due today. It will be submitted to Paramount in a few hours, when it is morning in L.A. The last changes are being made before it is faxed to meet the deadline.

October 23, 1989. Rome

Francis is excited, creative, and impatient in the throes of the production preparations while I deal with unexciting domestic problems. The apartment rented for our location stay was filthy. The cleaning lady worked half a day and left. My friend Paula came and helped me pack up seven cartons of the owner's personal junk. It was chilly, and the heater didn't work. Now several days have passed, and I have nearly gotten things in order; only the sink is stopped up. My domestic chores feel very frustrating to me but are completely insignificant in the life that surrounds me. Francis is facing the problem that, although he has rewritten the part many times to please Robert Duvall, every offer has been turned down. Now Francis must write him out of the script.

I find myself feeling my usual wave of location sadness, uprooted from my friends and my life at home, attending to the tasks, getting settled. But this is Rome, after all.

December 25, 1989. Rome

It is cold. There is a fire in the fireplace. The Christmas tree is shedding needles on the gray carpet. Francis is in bed listening to news in English on his shortwave radio. Roman and Sofia are asleep on the scruffy leather sofa. I am so completely happy they are here.

Last night, Christmas Eve, we went to Tally's (Talia Shire, Francis's sister) apartment. There is a huge terrace with views in every direction. She invited Al (Pacino) and Diane (Keaton), Andy (Garcia) and his family, and all of us. Francis's mother made traditional octopus sauce for the spaghetti. It was also Tally's son Robert's birthday. At 10:00 P.M. a group of us walked to the French Church for mass. I was anticipating hearing wonderful music resounding within the beautiful space. Instead, thin voices of the congregation evaporated in the arched nave. There were two memorable moments. One was when lights were turned on, dramatically illuminating the vast, elaborately painted ceiling and the extraordinary carvings above the altar. The second was when all the children came to the back, where I was sitting, and lit candles and formed a procession to carry a baby Jesus doll forward to the altar. As they stood holding their candles and fidgeting, waiting for the signal to begin,

304

Vogue, December, 1990

Quiet Flows the Don
Michael Corleone's life at the opera

(Above) *Godfather II and III;* (lower right) *the greatest fella of them all*

BY JOHN POWERS

FRANCIS FORD COPPOLA (HE'S RETURNED) his middle name for the occasion) has made a movie to argue about and dream on. Since I saw it, I've talked about little else — finding a rich texture of the characters, re-creating a few roles, redrawing scenes, speculating about the great stuff that Coppola obviously had to cut to reach a commercially viable running time. (I'd love to see the five-hour version.) This *Godfather* doesn't equal either of the first two, there are fewer transcendent moments, more clinkers, and the pacing feels both sluggish and rushed. Yet it's always absorbing, because Coppola's ambition is so grand and his conviction so genuine — like Part II, this movie revives what's come before. *Godfather III* may be disappointing when you're watching it, but in your head it's likely to start turning into a masterpiece — the conception, anyway, is nothing short of magisterial.

This means that Coppola's done better than I expected. I entered the theater dreading that he might betray two movies that are so much part of my life, I almost feel I've lived them; it would be hard for a 1990 sequel to live up to the originals, to above people's memories of them. When *The Godfather* and *The Godfather Part II* came out, during the Watergate years, they seemed to encapsulate a whole corrupt era when evil was done behind closed doors, politics and business appeared a higher species of gangsterism, and America was stained with the blood of its victims. (Say what you will against Nixon, he could get your adrenaline going.) Part III carries no such cultural urgency. Yet the original characters remain so fresh that, even 16 years after Part II, this film can incorporate them with startling ease. Kay (Diane Keaton), begs Michael to let their son quit law school and try his hand as an opera singer, while his bastard nephew Vincent (Andy Garcia), who's hot to join the family business, has a run-in with the dapper mobster Joey Zaza (an unnatural-seeming Joe Mantegna, who evidently thinks he's still starring in *American Buffalo*).

The opening half-hour is enjoyable but unnerving. Not only has the story lost the period...

...setting that was one key to the earlier films' alluring mood, but there's a lot of comedy, which led me to fear that the Corleones were about to be *Smurfed*. But the more merrily we re-live the changes in Michael: Decked out in peculiar, rather imperial-looking regalia, he's less imposing than we remember. His thickened face has gone baggy-eyed with a clear darkness to his lips, and his voice has grown more gravelly, in echo of his father's soft nothing so more aware that he lacks Vito's potent dignity — he has not become a ceremonious old man. Though now a legitimate businessman and richer than ever (he's able to give $100 million for charity work in Sicily), Michael seems to care, giant. And Pacino plays him as a slow, as times shuffling figure — almost comic, yet aching with a desire to forgive, too.

Ever dreaming of respectability, Michael is scheming to take over Immobiliare, a European conglomerate. Naturally, the other New York families want to wet their beaks, too. When Michael refuses, a flamboyant murder attempt is made against him (shades of the first *Godfather*, and the Corleones are plunged into conflict with the gravest and most treacherous ends in history: the back-room careers at the Vatican, whose cases connect them to the great Sicilian mob families and to the most ruthless and legitimized centers of Italian power. (All this is based on the actual late-'70s scandal at the Vatican Bank, whose corrupt dealings, some say, led to the murder of the hottest Pope John Paul I weeks after his election.) After decades of seeming to be assimilated, the Corleones return to Sicily for the second half of Part III.

This plot's tortuous twists aren't easy to follow, but the difficulty arises from half-deliberate. By Part II, the simple murders of Michael's much have already become the stuff of nostalgia; the glom and counterpoint of his business had grown so deadly elusive that many viewers got lost in Michael's dealings with Hyman Roth and Frankie Pantangeli. In Part III the conspiracies have grown even harder to unravel; they're as inviolable as the helicopter that blasts away at Michael and New York's other family heads as they meet in the glass-walled penthouse of an Atlantic City hotel.

What has always made the *Godfather* movies thrilling is their willingness to tackle a subject most movies and books are scared by: the mysteries of power — its seductiveness, its spiritual cost, the way it actually works on the actors and in the board room. To a man schooled in movie to gain money, Vito Corleone always decreed that Michael would become too a criminal but a respectable power, "the one to hold the strings." Michael's whole career has been torn by the effort to simultaneously go straight and pull all the strings, which also means manipulating the evil essential to his world. As Michael grows mired in increasingly obscure machinations — his enemies' and his own — he learns the futility of his attempts to keep power and be moral.

L.A. Weekly,
December 28, 1990—January 3, 1991

Paramount has $50 million riding on *The Godfather, Part III.* For Francis Ford Coppola, racked by self-doubt over the collapse of his Zoetrope Studios and still grief-stricken by the death of his son, the stakes are infinitely higher. But amid endless rewrites, on-set dramas, and spiraling budgets, Coppola is working his losses into a vision—maybe even a masterpiece. PETER J. BOYER reports from Sicily

Mary, quite contrary: When Coppola cast daughter, Sofia (opposite page), as Mary Corleone, it sparked an on-set revolution. Andy Garcia (above) plays her cousin—and heartthrob Vinnie.

Under the Gun

Vanity Fair, June 1990

DRAMA-LOGUE

FILM REVIEWS

Family members and friends of Michael Corleone (Al Pacino, third from left) gather in "The Godfather Part III"

Hollywood Drama-Logue, January 10–16, 1991

The stars who didn't make it to the mob

● *Frank Sinatra dropped out, cutting Madonna's role; Eddie Murphy asked in vain for a part*

Sunday Times (London), January 14, 1991

The Corleones Try to Go Straight In 'The Godfather Part III'

By JANET MASLIN

"The Godfather Part III," a valid and deeply moving continuation of the Corleone family saga, daringly holds forth the possibility of redemption. For Michael Corleone, now a tired, conscience-stricken patriarch, that means the chance to transcend the bloody sins that the first two "Godfather" films chronicled so unforgettably. For Francis Ford Coppola, who is back on familiar territory after many failures, noble and otherwise, it means the opportunity to regain a career's lost luster.

With Mr. Coppola's stately, ceremonious new "Godfather" epic, each of these men comes tantalizingly close to reversing his fortune. Of the two, Mr. Coppola comes closer.

Even now, Mr. Coppola apparently believes that the "Godfather" films are routine and unimaginative efforts by comparison with his flightier, more idiosyncratic pet projects (among them "Rumble Fish" and "One From the Heart"). That attitude is effectively a saving grace. It has allowed the "Godfather" films,

New York Times, December 25, 1990

The Godfather Part III

Directed by Francis Ford Coppola; written by Mario Puzo and Mr. Coppola; director of photography, Gordon Willis; edited by Barry Malkin, Lisa Fruchtman and Walter Murch; music by Carmine Coppola; production designer, Dean Tavoularis; produced by Francis Ford Coppola; released by Paramount Pictures. Running time: 161 minutes. This film is rated R.

Michael Corleone	Al Pacino
Kay Adams	Diane Keaton
Connie Corleone Rizzi	Talia Shire
Vincent Mancini	Andy Garcia
Don Altobello	Eli Wallach
Joey Zasa	Joe Mantegna
B. J. Harrison	George Hamilton
Grace Hamilton	Bridget Fonda
Mary Corleone	Sofia Coppola
Cardinal Lamberto	Raf Vallone
Anthony Corleone	Franc D'Ambrosio
Archbishop Gilday	Donal Donnelly
Dominic Abbandando	Don Novello
Don Tommasino	Vittorio Duse
Licio Lucchesi	Enzo Robutti
Lucy Mancini	Jeannie Linero

crime have been entirely in character during the intervening decades, but have simply neglected to turn up on screen.

mother of hot-blooded young Vincent Mancini (Andy Garcia), the Godfather of the future.

"The Godfather Part III," more frankly, mournfully operatic than its predecessors, is as haunted as a film about living characters can be. Casting the aging Michael in a Lear-like light, as a fading monarch worried about his children and the fate of his empire, it pointedly recalls the many losses in Michael's past (in this family-centered tragedy, there are echoes of Mr. Coppola's own history as well). Tempered by regret, Michael is now a much more fully drawn character than he had been, and Mr. Pacino's mesmerizing performance embodies many new shadings. The older Michael has lost none of his ruthlessness, but his confidence is shaky at times; so is his steely composure. More openly sentimental than before, Michael is now even capable of a fatherly twinkle or two.

The object of his affection is his daughter, Mary (Sofia Coppola), the coquettish head of the Corleone family's charitable foundation. The family's drive toward respectability now

The Corleones Return

Coppola didn't want to make another 'Godfather,' but an offer was made that he couldn't refuse. And now everyone wants to know: has he pulled it off?

BY JACK KROLL

The pressure is unbelievable," says Francis Ford Coppola. "This is just another movie. It's a Godfather movie. But it's become a big sporting event. It's about Francis—is he going to die or live?" In the last frantic days before the release of The Godfather Part III on Christmas Day, Coppola feels like a bull facing an army of matadors—the public that's been waiting for the next chapter in the Godfather saga for 16 years, since the release of the second Godfather in 1974. It's doubtful whether a movie director has ever felt this much pressure. Godfather I (1972) and its sequel were that rarity, a tremendous critical and box-office success that earned its studio, Paramount, a total of $800 million, plus nine Oscars and a permanent place in American culture.

For 15 years Coppola was besieged by successive regimes at Paramount, begging him to do a third Godfather. Always he refused, cracking that the only way he'd ever do it was as a farce, "Abbott and Costello Meet the Godfather." It was Paramount's current chairman, Frank

Mancuso, who finally broke down Coppola's resolve. After a succession of classically inane ideas of how to do a Coppola-less "Godfather," involving directors like Soviet expatriate Andrei Konchalovsky and actors like Sylvester Stallone and in the form of financial catastrophe that overwhelmed Coppola. A slew of box-office disappointments like "One from the Heart," "Tucker" Fish," "Gardens of Stone" and "Rumble Fish," forced the director into an apocalypse now of debts, litigation and bankruptcy. Man-cuso ambushed Coppola as neatly as Don Corleone waylaid his victims. A rat-tat-tat of dollars—$3 million to direct, $1 million to write the script, 15 percent of the box-office gross—and the deed was done.

Problems, problems: What followed was nearly a year of filming, in Rome, Sicily and New York, that made the problems of the first two "Godfathers" look like a makeup fix on a Pee-wee Herman movie. Budget Problems, starring a rise from the projected $44 million to $54 million. Casting Problems, starring the last-minute drafting of Coppola's inexperienced, 18-year-old daughter, Sofia, to replace an ill Winona Ryder. Most of all Coppola Problems, star-

ring a brilliant American director who couldn't understand why the gods kept singling him out for troubles and torments. "What is there about me that invites this controversy?" asks Coppola. "Why do I have to be an oddball on the edge of extinction? Why do people enjoy that?"

Between daily self-questionings in this Jobean vein, Coppola managed to finish his movie in time for the Christmas 1990 re-seeded. Coppola points out that meeting this deadline caused the kind of financial hemorrhaging that escalates budgets. Working with an "army of editors," he says, means that "we're paying maybe 50 times what it would cost if we could just mix with one editor." Plaintively he adds, "I started out saying 'I'm going to be a good boy. I'm going to do everything perfect. I'm going to work day and night.' And unavoidably I got tagged with my budgets going over. It's impossible to be a good boy." Mancuso bears out Coppola's self-defense. "No one was more responsible about the budget than Francis himself," he says. "He did everything possible to live up to it. I'm upset with the perception that he's irresponsible. It's absolutely untrue."

STEVE SANDS—OUTLINE

Newsweek, December 24, 1990

THE WHOLE *Godfather*

A WHITE CARD BEARING THE WORDS "WE'RE BACK WITH THE BORGIAS" IS TACKED TO THE DOOR OF FRANCIS COPPOLA'S OFFICE IN CINECITTA STUDIOS. THE LINE IS FROM THE SHOOTING SCRIPT OF *THE GODFATHER, PART III*, WHICH OPENS THIS MONTH, ALMOST EXACTLY A YEAR AFTER FILMING BEGAN, IN ROME. ❧ BEHIND COPPOLA'S MASSIVE DESK, A BULLETIN BOARD BEARS A PHOTOGRAPH OF THE JAPANESE DIRECTOR AKIRA KUROSAWA, A HISTORICAL CHART SHOWING ALL THE POPES, AND A LETTER FROM PARAMOUNT'S CHAIRMAN

THE FAMILY: COPPOLA WITH HIS PARENTS ON THE SET OF *THE GODFATHER, PART II*

The untold story of the making of the saga

BY PETER COWIE

Connoisseur, December 1990

Movies/David Denby

THE GRANDFATHER

JAN 7 1991 NEW YORK

" . . . Much of *The Godfather Part III* is grand yet muffled, [distant] from us and the first two films. Al Pacino performs brilliantly."

MOB STORY: *Godfather's Andy Garcia, Pacino.*

FOR MUCH OF ITS TWO-HOUR-AND-FORTY-[min]ute length, I waited for **The Godfa-ther Part III** to explode, and for a long [time] it only wheezed. The movie certainly [is] boring, but much of it is heavy-spirit-[ed] glum, as if the Mafia and the God-[movies] themselves had become un-[...] [important] facts of American [...] [admitting] neither levity nor excite-[ment]. [Mich]ael Corleone (Al Pacino), only [...] old in body and spirit, sets [...] hollow-eyed Pacino per-[...], but he appears to be [...] himself, and for a long time [...] with him. Fortunately, [...] [eventu]ally does come to life: [...] will become legendary. [...] Godfather (1972), the [...] piety and hair-[...]ished and enlarged [...] that were unsettling [...] [histo]ry of the Corleones' [...]rew us in, yet as [...] think that they [...] at they were vi-[...]uld kill some-[...] into bodies, the [...]rough windshields, re-[...]ur weak sentimentality. Francis [Cop]pola's story moved ahead fiercely yet with just enough space for texture and de-tail—for the interweaving of major and minor characters, foreground and back-ground, mob and America. The narrative possessed a fullness and decisiveness without equal in American movie history. *Part II* (1974) extended the Corleone family saga forward into Michael Cor-leone's unhappy maturity and the period of the family's control over Las Vegas in [the] fifties and sixties, and backward to [...] Corleone's youth in Sicily and Little [...]rly in the century. Though perhaps [...] exciting or as emotionally involving [...] first film, Godfather II was a work [...]essive high intelligence, a bitter [...]donic view of the corruption of [...] a and a frightening embodiment of [...] as a way of life.

[...]ther III renews the emotions es-[...] at the end of *Part II*—those mo-[...] which Michael, desolated by the [...] of his responsibilities and the [...] his crimes, grows increasingly [...] motionless in his lakeside Ne-[...]e. By 1979, a shrewd but self-[...]man, he's become sick of gang-

ster life. He has moved back to New York—a large apartment on Fifth Ave-nue—and has taken the Corleone family out of the rackets altogether. A financier, he buys himself respectability by contrib-uting millions to the Catholic church. *Part III* opens with a huge party, which match-es the wedding scene at the beginning of *The Godfather,* though without the bounding, sunshiny happiness. The party has the grayness of Michael's face. Pa-cino's hair is combed up, bristling; his brow is deeply furrowed. Hunched inside his rich man's business suit, he looks smaller, as if lifetime habits of calculation had shrunk his body.

Michael tries to buy a controlling inter-est (with Vatican approval) in an interna-tional conglomerate and runs afoul of an Italian Mr. Big, a corrupt financier misus-ing church funds. Set in the Vatican Bank and the Vatican itself, much of this in-trigue, resounding hollowly in the gloomy,

magnificent rooms, [...] yet muffled, distant [...] and from the first tw[o films.] Coppola and Mar[io Puzo] (who again collabor[ated on] the screenplay), sei[ze on] fresh real-life scandals [and ru-] mors (not just the S[indona] Affair but the surprisi[ng] death of John Paul I), w[e] have forgotten that th[ese] two films were about cr[ime] the American way of [busi-] ness, about a powerful [evil] preying on the corrupt[ibility] of the country. Suddenly [the] American theme is lost, [and] Coppola and Puzo are o[ff in] Rome remaking *The Sho[es of]* *the Fisherman.* A lot of [the] screenplay is overexplicit [and] stiff—lazy—and the hus[hed] solemnity gets a little th[ick.] The movie needs someo[ne] like manic Joe Pesci fr[om] *GoodFellas* scamperi[ng] across the marbled floors [in] its self-esteem.

Nothing quite commands u[s] emotionally. Michael's sister [Con-] nie (Talia Shire), slinks i[n] and out, a fierce witch in black, [plot-] plotting murders. Kay (Diane [Keaton),] though remarried, ex-periences a mild return of affection for Mi-chael. (So what?) His son, Anthony (Franc [D'Ambrosio]), wants to become an opera singer and rejects his dad, but he's no more than a sweet-faced cipher. In a catastrophic decision, Coppola, ever his own Godfather, cast his daughter Sofia as Michael's daugh-ter Mary (the talented Winona Ryder had dropped out). Miss Coppola has a thick, curled upper lip that she doesn't have the training and technique to use as an actress. She appears raw and unprotected, naked al-most, and since she has a flat, uninflected voice as well, the exposure is complete. When the rising young hood Vincenzo (Andy Garcia), the bastard son of Michael's brother Sonny, and a dangerously attractive man, falls in love with her, we are baffled. His semi-incestuous desire for her is meant to be the mainspring of the plot, but the spring isn't wound.

Michael seeks redemption. But like all movie gangsters, he's pulled back into

New York, January 7, 1991

PARAMOUNT PICTURES PRESENTA UNA PRODUCCION
Francis Ford Coppola
El Padrino 2ª PARTE

Technicolor

DISTRIBUIDA POR
Cinema International Corporation

The Godfather Part III

Recapturing the Myth

By Marilyn Moss
Associate Editor

WHEN MICHAEL CORLEONE sat enshrined in his own psychic bankruptcy at the close of "The Godfather Part II" in 1974, it seemed that Francis Ford Coppola had closed the book on one of film history's most luminous episodes. Having already inscribed both Michael and the Corleone family deep into the mainstream of our American mythos, it would have seemed preposterous to some filmgoers even to imagine that Coppola could go any further with his saga of this Italian-American family. To do so would be nothing short of tempting the fates, let alone his own muse. He had already dared and succeeded in doing the impossible: taking his enormously successful "The Godfather"—at the time, the largest grossing film ever—and crafting a sequel that was to some even more compelling and more richly woven in psychological tension than the original.

Even in making "The Godfather Part II," Coppola could only have been painfully aware of the stakes at hand; he was in fact tampering with a mythic monster of a film that had already become larger than him, had already escaped into the culture with a life of its own. Given these odds, we can only wonder what pressures he must be feeling now, 16 years later, as he prepares to send his third installment, "The Godfather Part III," into the wilderness of a vastly changed film audience. This third "Godfather," as we all know, is the film Coppola has always refused to make.

It is no overstatement to say that filmgoers have been begging for more "Godfather" since 1974. If we have not been telling each other outright, then we have all been guilty of those fantasies we've secreted: our personal scenarios of the narrative direction the third "Godfather" would take if there were to be one. This testifies to the

enormity of the "Godfather" myth. It is also a subject that hasn't escaped Fred Roos and Gray Frederickson, two of the producers of "The Godfather Part III." Roos, also producer of "The Godfather Part II" as well as nearly every other of Coppola's major films, and Frederickson, producer of "The Godfather" and "The Godfather Part II," have been with Coppola on and off in Italy for the past year to see this production through its various stages. They both know Coppola intimately and recently were willing to sit down for an exclusive interview with BOXOFFICE for some talk about the latest chapter of Coppola's epic story of the Corleone family.

While Frederickson has worked with Coppola on a less consistent basis than has Roos, he is nonetheless quite familiar with the tension that mounts for everyone before a "Godfather" film is

released. As for Roos, he first became associated with Coppola in 1968, at the time the director had just completed his first major film, "You're A Big Boy Now." Their first meetings took place, oddly enough, when Coppola called him, as Roos puts it, "simply to pick my brain" and to talk about different actors. Then a casting director, Roos says now that the telephone conversations weren't supposed to lead to anything in particular—however, they certainly did. At the time, Coppola was casting his 1969 film, "The Rain People," and when he got the first "Godfather" job a few years later, he asked Roos to cast it for him; in Roos' words, Coppola "hired me without ever seeing me."

When Roos and Coppola started out doing the first "Godfather," neither was particularly attracted to a Mafia story, Roos says, nor was either of them thinking in terms of epic storytelling. So, how did the movie take on the proportions it did? Roos is quick to say that Coppola could only have done it by transforming it beyond its original potential. "It couldn't have sustained his interest if he had done it in a more direct way," he adds. And here, Frederickson makes a good point: "It's the idea of family—the kind of family Francis knows best, the Italian-American immigrant experience." Both agree that Coppola's meditations on family have contributed to the enormous popularity of the "Godfather" films. Perhaps they are implying another important fact: American movie-goers have somehow seen themselves and their own families in the Corleone clan.

Yet several other things happened when the first "Godfather" was released. Contrary to popular word, the Mafia wasn't upset about Maria Puzo's book or about the movie. In fact, they

Boxoffice, October 1990

IT AIN'T OVER TILL THE FAT MAN DIRECTS

BY IVOR & SALLY OGLE DAVIS

Francis Coppola and the making of *The Godfather Part III*: A very grand opera in three acts

ACT ONE

The curtain rises on a bucolic vineyard. Upstage, rows of tender green vines stretch into the distance. Stage right, an old barn housing the small family winery stands weathered by the sun. In the foreground, center stage, on a wooden veranda, an aging Don, disheveled, his dark beard streaked with white, wearing a rumpled cotton suit, sits in a Victorian wicker chair surrounded by his family.

He is sad. As the overture fades, he sings of his regrets: his youthful profligacy, followed by too few successes, his waning power and his enemies who are even now trying to wrest control of his family, his empire, even his beloved vineyard.

A servant enters and announces that a delegation has arrived from a far-off region known as Perra Mount. They enter wearing Armani suits and sporting ponytails. Over a glass of the Don's finest Niebaum-Coppola, they plead their case.

Twice, Don Francisco di Coppola has saved their skins, pouring 800 million lire into their beleaguered coffers, spoils from the two previous "wars" he has waged at their behest. Now, vacillating leadership and poor investments have laid them open to overthrow. One member of the delegation tearfully spills out their plight in a

ILLUSTRATION BY ROB WESTERBERG

Los Angeles Magazine, December 1990

MOVIES

WHY WE'RE MARRIED TO THE MOB

By Michael Sragow

Francis Coppola himself couldn't have drummed up more anticipation for the late-1990 release of *The Godfather, Part III* than the fusillade of gangster films that strafed theaters this summer and fall. The 1930s and 1940s cartoon grotesques of *Dick Tracy*, the roaring-1920s racketeers and political bosses in *Miller's Crossing*, the swingin' English sadists

who are *The Krays*, the contemporary mafiosi of *The Freshman*, and Martin Scorsese's *GoodFellas*—they're all, in some way, the godchildren of Coppola and Mario Puzo, and their mythic creation, Don Vito Corleone.

When *The Godfather* came out in 1972 and *The Godfather, Part II* arrived a couple of years later, the story of Don Corleone grooming his youngest son for a lawful career—only to see him take over the Don's criminal empire—was justly acclaimed for elevating the American gangster movie to a peak of tragic irony. Using his education cold-bloodedly, Michael Corleone regularized the family business. His methods dramatized Puzo's thesis (never stated outright in the film)—"a lawyer with a briefcase can steal more money than a thousand men with guns." But many of the college kids who recited favorite bits of dialogue from both *Godfather* movies took the Corleone saga as a design for living instead of an

alarming reality. *I made him an offer he couldn't refuse* might serve as the motto for all money-grabbers who came of age in the '80s. How different was the art of the deal from the Corleones' art of the steal?

The cynicism that the *Godfathers* exposed became a given in crime movies (*Scarface, Once Upon a Time in America*) and TV series (*Miami Vice, Crime Story, Wiseguy*). But genres are like sharks; they've got to keep moving or they die. No matter how *The Godfather, Part III* turns out, Coppola's rejection of already-exhausted subjects for his latest film is admirable. Early scripts that Coppola dismissed for the third *Godfather* reported-

ly covered such familiar topics as drug cartels, CIA hits, and vendettas. And in Coppola's own script, according to *Daily Variety*, "Michael Corleone seeks to legitimize the Corleone fortune by acquiring a stake in a European multinational real estate concern, with the Vatican as intermediary." It's a piquant idea—the unified Europe of the '90s as America's new frontier.

In *Miller's Crossing*, the Coen Brothers (*Blood Simple, Raising Arizona*) aren't nearly as ambitious or provocative. Their film is self-consciously intricate and "intellectual"—which makes it a natural for opening night of the New York Film Festival. The Coens (Joel directs, Ethan produces; both write) bring nothing fresh to their gangster-movie gamesmanship; they also lack old-fashioned "heart." They aim no higher than to up the ante on post-*Godfather* pessimism: City officials shift their favors openly from one crime boss to another; the police are hired guns.

The movie hinges on the rivalry between an Irish chieftain (Albert Finney) and an Italian kingpin (Jon Polito); the antihero is the Irishman's right-hand man, Tom (Gabriel Byrne), who bounces between the two mobs. Unlike Coppola, who views the Corleones as figures out of "a Shakespeare play about a royal family," the Coens see their gangsters as fall guys, not tragic heroes. Tom is merely the man behind the man, content to be an invisible, shrewd adviser. He can't be tragic because

> *I made him an offer he couldn't refuse might serve as the motto for all money-grabbers who came of age in the '80s.*

he does not have far enough to drop. It's as if Coppola had constructed *The Godfather* around Tom Hagen.

Perhaps, in their own smarter-than-thou way, the Coens tried to create a fantasy figure for a bureaucratic age. But only a Kafka-

> **The Corleones now arouse laughs (not shocks) of recognition.**

Esquire, October 1990

BRAVOS & BLOOD

"The Godfather, Part III" features Al Pacino as Michael Corleone, left, Sofia Co

The Corleone family turns to Rome for legitimacy and power in symphonic 'Godfather, Part III'

By Duane Byrge
Enterainment News Wire

It's business, and personal. A complex depiction of Michael Corleone's dying-days attempt to cement the family in the "legitimate" business world and attain spiritual redemption, this third installment of the Corleone Family chronicle is a full-bodied, albeit somber dramatic orchestration.

However, legitimacy has its price — respectability exacts a grayness and a tempering of one's style and substance — and this splendidly conceived, although often confusing saga, is itself vulnerable to the dramatic doldrums of Michael's venture into "respectable" dominions.

"The Godfather, Part III" does not go to the mattresses, it goes to the boardroom, and mainstream viewers after being served up several early-scene courses of the Byzantine world of international commerce will yearn for more old-Corleone action. Francis Ford Coppola's splendidly symphonic tale, although certainly not devoid of fire works and cannons, is a more subdued, legato movement.

While it will be no revelation to sophisticated viewers that the Vatican's temporal, big-business side has swum in some very muddy moral waters, it's hard not to expect outrage over the film's content, as the Catholic Church lays down here with the mob and, in this case, proves itself to be the less honorable partner.

"The Godfather, Part III" is more a character study than a "gangster" movie. It's a brilliant portrait of the now-elderly Michael Corleone's (Al Pacino) desperate efforts to atone for his life of crime and his most haunting transgression, the murder of his brother Fredo. He barges into good works and charity — he

MOVIE REVIEW

The Godfather, Part III
Rated R. Opens Tuesday at the Marina Pacifica, Long Beach; Hi-Way 39 Drive-In, Westminster.

bestows $100 million to the Catholic Church for his beloved Sicily — but, more than anything, he's obsessed with leaving his family on high, "legitimate" grounds, severing all business ties with the other "families." As such, this third-part "Godfather" is substantively the saga's dramatic denouement, a post-climactic wrap-up of the Corleone crime years and a turn in a new direction.

Mario Puzo and Francis Ford Coppola's shrewd and character-sensitive screenplay is a grand-scale distillation of fact-based materials as Michael Corleone enters into a clandestine pact with the Vatican to win control of the world's largest conglomerate, of which the church holds a 25 percent voting interest. Necessarily, such a narrative necessitates numerous static scenes — stockholder meetings, PR functions, etc. — and "Godfather III" sometimes bloats under this gray ceremonial pomp. Michael Corleone now has his "war lawyers" fight his battles.

"Godfather III's" suit-coated side, however, is spectacularly juiced up, fortunately, when Michael's old-world foes reappear — ties he can't shake. The film is at its most exciting in these violent, confrontational scenes, with Michael's "nephew," Sonny's illegitimate son (Andy Garcia), flexing the family's muscle, a role that the honored Michael has abdicated. Unfortunately, the film's cross-cut, highly-choreographed finale may prove somewhat incomprehensible to mainstream viewers as

Press-Telegram, December 21, 1990

Cinema

Schemes and Dreams for Christmas

On Santa's list: a Mafia don, a Master of the Universe and a De Niro Oscar?

Christmas films come in two basic shapes: books and toys. The toys—doll babies like *Home Alone* and cuddly creatures like *Edward Scissorhands*—may mop up at the box office. But prestige is a Hollywood product too; it can be cashed in for Oscars if enough critics and Motion Picture Academy voters are impressed by what they see. So lauded literary properties like *Hamlet* and *The Sheltering Sky* become ambitious films. Herewith, three bookish films hoping for a shelf life that extends past New Year's:

THE GODFATHER PART III

They were like the Kennedys of Massachusetts, an immigrant clan that reaped power and pain in almost equal measure. They were like the Ewings of *Dallas*, with a brilliant, scheming son wrapping his dirty deals in a whisper and a smile. They were like every family, the Corleones of Mario Puzo's imagination, except they wrote their quarrels in blood. They killed their rivals, and when they felt betrayed from within, they killed each other.

How titillating the Corleones seemed in 1972 and '74, when Francis Ford Coppola turned Puzo's best seller into two Oscar-winning *Godfather* films. Here was a family of murderers viewed with cool compassion; they did their lurid business with style. Coppola's own style, which set the tone for '70s movies, was called operatic—meaning that the characters moved slowly, died grandly and emoted at the top of their lungs. The book was a fast, brutal read; the movie saga was an extended, ravishing look.

And now, at long last, a long look back in *The Godfather Part III*, a meandering but finally quite affecting climax to the saga. It is 1979, and Michael Corleone (Al Pacino), the sleek, ruthless don, has become a legitimate billionaire. His sister Connie (Talia Shire) has dredged herself out of a sullen stupor to become his feisty adviser. His ex-wife Kay (Diane Keaton) has remarried. His son Anthony (Franc D'Ambrosio) has eyes to become an opera singer. His daughter Mary (Sofia Coppola) is itching to grow up and fall in love.

At first Michael is pleased to have his crimson career behind him. When Vincent Mancini (Andy Garcia), the bastard son of Michael's brother Sonny, shows up ready to bite the ear off any idle Mafioso, Michael tells him. "I don't need tough guys. I need more lawyers." But in his negotiations with a crafty padrone (Eli Wallach), with a gaudy capo (Joe Mantegna), even with some slippery Vatican officials over a European real estate deal, Michael decides he needs tough guys. The question is: Can he still be tough enough to lead them?

That's not a tough question. *The Godfather Part III*, is a gangster picture, after all,

and Michael is the antihero with whom the series lives and dies. The true perplexer is whether filmgoers will care to see, or care about, an aging entrepreneur haunted by specters from films nearly two decades old. Because this is a movie about loss, Pacino must relinquish the steely calm of his youthful Michael; now he is Lear without the grandeur. Nor can *G3* find suave new twists and characters to propel the plot and lure the teens. Garcia, an electric actor, swaggers so handsomely that he makes one wish for another sequel. But he is helpless to strike sparks with Sofia Coppola (the director's daughter), whose gosling gracelessness comes close to wrecking the movie.

The first *Godfather* films sketched a history of the Mafia as a cracked-mirror reflection of American industry. One hoped *G3* might pit the Corleones against the bad boys of the drug trade: the old Italians vs. blacks and Hispanics, rustic chivalry vs. cutthroat capitalism. Instead, Coppola, who wrote the screenplay with Puzo, sends Michael on a side trip to Rome and Sicily.

There is some colorful conniving: who'd have guessed that an international cartel fatally poisoned Pope John Paul I? But *G3* never persuades one of the urgency of its maxim that "finance is a gun, and politics is knowing when to pull the trigger." With all its boardroom bickering, the plot is a gun that shoots mostly blanks. *G3* is too faithful to the deliberate pacing of the first two films: the slow walking into a dark room, the silence surrounding the threats. For two hours the movie labors up the winding path of its story, wheezing like an old man who won't admit his age.

But fidelity has its rewards. Remember how, in the other *Godfathers*, nearly every religious ceremony (baptism, festival, funeral) is accompanied by a murder? As in the first film, *G3* has a spectacular payoff: accounts of honor settled with elaborate

76

TIME, DECEMBER 24, 1990

Time, December 24, 1990

An offer Coppola couldn't refuse

ON LOCATION

PETER COWIE reports from Rome on the making of Godfather III

Francis Ford Coppola is back this week doing what he does best – directing Godfather movies.

The $44m production of Godfather III, the movie he said he'd never make, has now lumbered through two months of principal photography here at Cinecittà, just outside Rome, and Coppola grandly predicts it will be "the cathedral of Godfather movies". Looking fitter and more relaxed than he has in years, Coppola seems to have re-inserted himself effortlessly into the saga of the Corleone family, which he began chronicling exactly 20 years ago.

And with good reason. The seven hours and 30 minutes of celluloid comprising Godfathers I and II has become an industry unto itself. The films have grossed more than $700m worldwide and have earned an additional $100m in TV and video.

Together, the two represent a milestone in contemporary film-making – artistic triumphs that translated into box-office triumphs. Steven Spielberg recently called The Godfather "the last great movie" of the present generation of film-makers. And The Godfather Part II is widely heralded as the greatest sequel of all time.

Despite this acclaim, the process of tooling up Godfather III has consumed 15 years and several million dollars in development funds. More than any film in recent history, Godfather III became a corporate obsession. So intense was the passion to get it afloat that both Charles Bludorn, founder of Gulf & Western (now Paramount), and Michael Eisner, one-time Paramount production chief and now head of Disney, each took a stab at writing a story for the film, along with literally dozens of professional writers who also contributed scripts and treatments along the way.

● *The son also rises: Al Pacino as Michael Corleone in Godfather II*

Sylvester Stallone was signed to star and direct at one point but the deal blew apart at the eleventh hour. Eddie Murphy even called Mario Puzo, author of the original book, and Coppola, to tell them he'd like a role in the project, if they'd just give him a script.

Godfather III has remained a great beached whale – a symbol of corporate frustration.

What happened to change all that? Francis Coppola recalls a phone call he received from Frank Mancuso last year in which the Paramount president tried one final time to get the project moving. This time Mancuso promised that the studio was prepared to make the film "his way". Previous screenplays over the years had focused on assassinations of Latin American dictators, hits by CIA operatives and random vendettas among rival families. Coppola wanted to concentrate instead on the character of Michael Corleone, the youngest son of the Don, played by Al Pacino, who unwillingly inherits the mantle of his father, played by Marlon Brando – "because that's where the tragedy lies". Michael's story had been lost in most of Paramount's discarded scripts, Coppola observed.

"I told Paramount that for $40,000 my people and I would prepare a feasibility study," Coppola recalls. "At the end of a couple of months Paramount would get an outline, a budget, a schedule and a list of who would appear in the movie."

Coppola and Puzo began work on the script for Godfather III last April. By the start

Continued on page 4

Sunday Times (London), January 14, 1991

MOB CONTROL

It was an offer I couldn't refuse: a chance to work with America's biggest director, a front-row seat to a Mafia hit, and all the pastries I could eat. I was an extra on the set of 'Godfather III'.

"DO YOU WANNA BE AN extra in *The Godfather III*?"

My production assistant friend, in lieu of buying me groceries, had just made me an offer I couldn't refuse.

I'm an Alabama-raised, struggling screenwriter who recently moved to New York in order to starve to death. "Struggling" is a word used in the film industry to describe someone who does something related to film work, but who isn't *really* doing it because his talent has yet to generate a paycheck. (I've got an argument against this school of thought — if making money is the only way to legitimize a talent, then the only people in America who are really having sex are prostitutes. *Hmmm.*) The "extra" — which I was about to become — is a struggling *actor* who's willing to be herded into a large room at 6:00 a.m. with 500 other struggling actors and wait for that golden moment when he will get to run, screaming, out of camera range, while a stuntman fires a machine gun into the air. I know what you're thinking. If extras are getting paid for their work, then they aren't struggling. Well, by that criterion you've got me, but the truly demeaning nature of the whole thing makes it a struggle by default. It sounded like fun, though. It also sounded like $50 a day plus breakfast.

To be honest, even without the enticement of a free cheese Danish I would've jumped at the chance to be in a *Godfather* picture. Wouldn't you? *Godfathers I* and *II*

Joe Mantegna relaxes moments before being rubbed out on the set of *Godfather III*.

BY PAUL TATARA

are the best gangster films ever made. The epic tale of olive-oil magnate Vito Corleone and his progeny of pistol-packin' paisans (writers love alliteration) established Francis Ford Coppola as the rarest breed of director — the bankable visionary. Coppola's blood-filled opera of ruthless brass-ring chasing resulted, ironically enough, in his own realization of the American Dream. He reveled in his newfound power. He put up a great deal of his own money to start Zoetrope Studios. He even published a magazine. He never got into the olive-oil business, but you get the picture. The whiz kid was definitely here to stay.

Then came the slide. After the flawed, but mostly brilliant, *Apocalypse Now* (1979), Coppola (the visionary) created jewels like *The Outsiders* (1983), *Rumble Fish* (1983), *One from the Heart* (1982) and "Life Without Zoe," his indefensible contribution to 1989's *New York Stories* trilogy, which stands as the single most nauseating experience of my generally nausea-enriched life. At this point in his career, the siren call of *Godfather III* (to be released on Christmas day) must have sounded sweet to Coppola. I had to wonder, though, if the man could possibly spark enough passion to pull off another movement of the *Godfather* story. Whether

US NOVEMBER 12, 199

---

left, holding the Italian sausage sandwich. That's the girl who wouldn't go out with me on the right.) The ensuing carnage can only be described as "Sicilian." Neato. Let's do it!

Okay, as soon as we set up the camera. Coppola's cinematographer, as on the other *Godfather* pictures, is Gordon Willis (who also shot the unspeakably gorgeous black-and-white vistas in Woody Allen's *Manhattan*) is roundly praised by critics and filmmakers alike as a genius, but, genius or not, watching him set up a shot is akin to watching Mother Nature form a canyon. It looks like something might be going on, but you're not really sure what, and you won't be seeing the end result for a few years anyway.

Willis growls, slouches like he's heading towards Bethlehem, and holds that little viewer-thingy that dangles on a string around his neck up to his eye. Then he mutters something about "light" and "s—."

While he spends two hours or so scaring the extras, his assistants hang massive tarps across the street to block out the sunlight and give the shot a more natural look. My question is, if they want it to look natural, why don't they just turn on the camera and screw the tarps? I don't say anything, though, because Willis looks like he could be provoked. I picture myself being beaten senseless with his little viewer-thingy.

THEN A SHOCKING THING happens. Looking for a clear path in case Willis lunges, I turn to my right and see, looming over me in the middle of Prince Street, the monolith from Stanley Kubrick's *2001: A Space Odyssey*. The hair stands up on the back of my neck as its shadow falls across me. I can't breathe. It stands about five feet ten inches tall, wears a beard, glasses, and is draped in a rumpled, gray linen suit.

"No . . . wait . . . oh — it's just Coppola. And he's *big*. Ark big. The man has reportedly lost millions of dollars in the years since he made *One from the Heart*, but the money he's saved has obviously been spent on cannoli. This is the first time I've seen him, since he spends most of his time tucked away in a big silver camper at the far end of the set. The camper (which he calls "Silverfish") supposedly contains endless rows of video monitors, a full kitchen, and a Jacuzzi. I can picture him in the kitchen (rubbing his hands maniacally as the Prego bubbles away on the back burner), but a Jacuzzi Isn't that a little . . . California-ish? Even Fredo Corleone wouldn't have gotten into a Jacuzzi . . . and

It's a hit: On the streets of Little Italy, Joe Mantegna models the latest in Mafia couture, the bullet-riddled overcoat (above). After being blown away by gun-toting spectators, he lies dying in the street (below).

---

he could or not, I wanted to be there to experience the guns, the sausage, the MAGIC! But first, as an extra, I had to experience the holding area.

If a director is a wealthy rancher and the extras are cattle, then the holding area is the barn. *Godfather III's* barn during the days that I worked was in the Puck Building on Lafayette Street in SoHo. (You can tell it's the Puck Building because there's a really nice statue out front of Mickey Rooney wearing a diaper.) The holding area within is really just a cavernous, folding-chair-strewn room, where all 500 extras congregate in the morning to change into costumes, put on makeup, eat sugar-bomb pastries (good Danish!), and fall back asleep since it's 6:30 a.m. and you're not really going to be doing anything till 10:00 or 11:00 anyway. The life of an extra can be fairly exciting when a scene is actually being shot, but, as Tom Petty says, the waiting is the hardest part. And wait you do. For hours. From what I could determine, the more experienced extras have developed two predominant ways to pass the time between takes . . .

ONE THE GRIPE I wasn't as good at this as some of the old hands, and I think I have a certain gift for complaining. Strictly speaking, The Gripe consists of walking around the holding area and talking in a loud voice to anyone who'll listen about how you're a *real* actor, and who the hell do these wardrobe guys think they are?

The "Old Pro" Gripe is the one preferred by four out of five experts. This subcategory is best exemplified by a meeting of the minds, which I had my first morning on the set. I'm sitting there at 7:00 a.m., my head slowly rocking on its axis, when a balding man in a white shirt and ugly brown tie sits down next to me.

"Redford's always blowing his lines," he says.

"Huh?"

"Redford always blows his lines."

For a second this sounds like some sort of spy code to me, as if I'm supposed to whisper a cryptic counter-code and he'll slide documents into my hand.

"At least he blew 'em when I worked on *Condor*."

That's something else. Extras like to shorten movie titles. If you're going to drop *Prizzi's Honor* into a conversation, just call it *Prizzi's*. If you've had a role in a one-word-titled film like *Gotcha!*, you shorten it to the point that you don't mention it at all . . . which, if you've ever

Married to the Mob: After suffering financial failure with films like *One from the Heart* and *Tucker*, Coppola hopes to clean up with the second sequel to his Oscar-winning epic about the Corleones.

CHAPTER 22

The Rivals

*T*HE GODFATHER dominated the movie scene in 1972, the year it appeared. *The Godfather Part II* equally overshadowed the film scene in 1974. Considering the public acclaim that was heaped upon them—and the press attention that greeted *Godfather Part III* in 1990—it might be thought there was no worthy competition. That is not quite true. Hollywood produced a number of exemplary films in those three years. It is interesting to examine them with an eye to their links with *The Godfather*.

Michael Caine and Laurence Olivier in *Sleuth*

Liza Minnelli in *Cabaret*

1972

SLEUTH:
Coppola wanted the greatest actor in the world, which meant Olivier or Brando. Since Olivier was ill, Brando became Coppola's target. After his recovery, Olivier appeared in the screen version of the successful stage thriller *Sleuth*. Its musical score also was a nominee for an Oscar that year, in competition with the one from *The Godfather*.

CABARET:
This film of Berlin in the early Thirties, directed by Bob Fosse and starring Liza Minnelli as singer Sally Bowles, won a brace of Oscars the same year that *The Godfather* won its share. Coppola lost the Best Director Oscar in '72 to Bob Fosse, and his sister, Talia, lost the Best Actress Oscar to Liza Minnelli at the same ceremony.

THE EMIGRANTS:
The Godfather family was founded by an emigrant from Sicily. The family in *The Emigrants* leaves famine-stricken 19th-century Sweden and builds a homestead in Minnesota. Unlike the Corleones, they are law-abiding folk. Also unlike *The Godfather*, this forceful epic is overlong.

SOUNDER:
Like *The Godfather*, *Sounder* is a period piece. It takes place during the Great Depression. The black sharecroppers in the deep South endure their

tribulations, as the Mafia family in New York endure theirs (although the Mafia eventually rose above them through violence). The sharecropper family headed by Paul Winfield is as close as the Sicilian one headed by Marlon Brando.

THE RULING CLASS:

In 1962 when producer Sam Spiegel set out to make *Lawrence of Arabia,* he offered the role to Marlon Brando. When Brando passed, Spiegel chose an unknown young actor named Peter O'Toole to play Lawrence. Ten years later, O'Toole appeared as a mad son of British royalty who thinks he is God in *The Ruling Class.* Based on an overlong satirical play, it has brilliant moments.

LADY SINGS THE BLUES:

Don Corleone invites an assassination attempt when he refuses to traffic in drugs. It is drugs that bring disaster to the life of Blues singer Billie Holiday in this old-fashioned biography with new-fangled drugs, sex, and squalor. Diana Ross played Billie Holiday in *Lady Sings The Blues,* which also featured an inspired new comedian named Richard Pryor.

TRAVELS WITH MY AUNT:

Based on a Graham Greene novel, the film is about a staid bank accountant who is landed in a series of adventures by his life-loving aunt. *The Godfather* is a novel about an Ivy League college boy who is landed in a series of adventures by his life-loving father. *Travels with My Aunt* is a fairly disastrous adaptation of a delightful novel, while *The Godfather* is a triumphant adaptation of another one.

DELIVERANCE:

Like *The Godfather,* this film derived from a bestselling novel is an apocalyptic vision of man's inhumanity. Four men spend a weekend canoeing down a dangerous river, and find the real peril to their lives is from other humans. James Dickey wrote the screenplay from his novel, and actors Burt Reynolds and Jon Voight made this a thrilling adventure.

Robert Redford in *The Candidate*

THE CANDIDATE:

Paramount had wanted Robert Redford for the role of Michael Corleone, but he found a more felicitous role in *The Candidate*. This film, about a young WASP who runs for Congress, takes as cynical an attitude toward politicians as does *The Godfather*.

THE HEARTBREAK KID:

As his agent tried to negotiate a higher fee, Charles Grodin lost his chance at stardom when Dustin Hoffman was chosen to play *The Graduate*. Grodin finally made it five years later in the delicious romp, *The Heartbreak Kid*. Neil Simon wrote the hilarious screenplay.

PLAY IT AGAIN, SAM:

Paramount covered all the bases in 1972, featuring drama with *The Godfather*, and comedy with *Play It Again, Sam*. This product of Woody Allen strove for the macho image that the Corleones had as birthright.

1974

MURDER ON THE ORIENT EXPRESS:

Talia lost her Best Supporting Actress Oscar to Ingrid Bergman, who made a cameo appearance among a dozen other stars in *Murder*.

Charles Grodin and Cybill Shepherd in *The Heartbreak Kid*

. . . Agatha Christie's Hercule Poirot solves a murder on a snowbound train in this elegant version of a classic mystery novel. Unfortunately, as soon as the train chugs into its snowdrift, the film stops moving too.

LENNY:

Lenny Bruce never garroted anyone or shot him dead. His troubles with the law flowed from his allegedly obscene monologues. *Lenny* is an old-fashioned rags-to-riches-to-rags story, as *The Godfather* is a rags-to-riches-to-ruin story. Dustin Hoffman of the Pacino-De Niro-Hoffman axis starred.

CHINATOWN:

This movie's crime did not originate in a play, a book, or a stand–up comedy routine. In the Thirties, a Los Angeles private eye burrows into a simple case until it leads to murder and scandal. The star of *Chinatown*, Jack Nicholson,

Woody Allen directed/wrote/starred in *Play It Again, Sam*

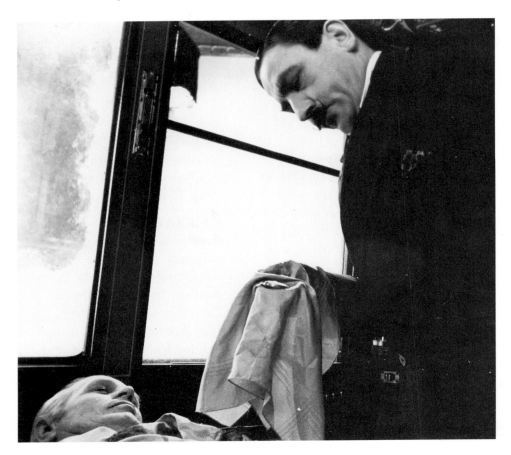

Agatha Christie's *Murder on the Orient Express*

Jack Nicholson and Faye Dunaway in *Chinatown*

had been considered for the role of Michael Corleone, but Coppola felt he needed someone who looked Italian. *Chinatown* shows that crooked politicians exist on the other coastline too.

ALICE DOESN'T LIVE HERE ANYMORE:

A widow sets off with her young son for Monterey and a singing career. The film offers a realistically squalid but endearing look at a slice of America today. Its director, Martin Scorsese,

referred Robert De Niro to Coppola for *Godfather Part II,* based on his performance in Scorsese's gripping *Mean Streets.*

THE CONVERSATION:

A bugging-device expert who lives only for his work finally develops a conscience. This absorbing, timely (in view of Watergate) Kafkaesque suspense story was both written and directed by Francis Coppola. He and leading actor Gene Hackman had a field day. It

also features John Cazale, who played Fredo Corleone and Frederic Forrest, who starred in other Coppola films.

THE TOWERING INFERNO:

A newly-constructed, high-rise hotel is destroyed by fire. A showmanlike but padded disaster epic, *The Towering Inferno*'s cast of stars is impressive, as opposed to the relative unknowns surrounding Brando in the original *Godfather. The*

Ellen Burstyn in *Alice Doesn't Live Here Anymore*

Towering Inferno is worth seeing for its sheer old-fashioned expertise and special effects.

DAY FOR NIGHT:
Day for Night, directed and written by Francois Truffaut, who also appeared in the film, describes the friction and personality clashes that beset the making of a film in Nice. It offers an immensely enjoyable insider's view of the goings-on in the making of a movie. *Day for Night* is as enjoyable as Eleanor Coppola's documentary on her husband's tumultuous shoot of *Apocalypse Now.* Similarly, several written biographies of Francis Coppola describe the

Francois Truffaut's *Day For Night*

frictions that beset the making of *The Godfather*.

1990

GOODFELLAS:
This film offers another look at the Mafia, starring, inevitably, Robert De Niro in a film directed by Martin Scorsese, based on a book by Nicholas Pileggi. Critics again blanched at the brutality, but the film's overall tone is more playful than that of *The Godfather*.

REVERSAL OF FORTUNE:
Again the subject is murder, but this time it focuses on the effort of a brilliant criminal lawyer, Alan Dershowitz, and his young associates, to defend an accused wife slayer.

GHOST:
In this film, the murder victim comes back from the Great Beyond to seek justice. No criminal lawyer or Godfather are there to help. A black psychic and the victim's love and ingenuity must pull it off.

MISERY:
James Caan returns as a victim rather than a hot-headed gunman. Talk about sadism and brutality! Actress Kathy Bates kills and maims

with impunity until the final reel in this screen version of the Stephen King novel.

THE GRIFTERS:
Showing the light-fingered end of the criminal spectrum, this film is more like *The Sting* than *The Godfather*. Again, it's all in the family, albeit with a whiff of incest, as mother and son are grifters hostile to one another.

PRETTY WOMAN:
There's little talk of prostitution in *The Godfather*, to avoid harming the atmosphere of nobility. But *Pretty Woman* features a most engaging prostitute, played by Julia Roberts, set in the Beverly Wilshire Hotel.

POSTCARDS FROM THE EDGE:
This film's novelistic source was written by Carrie Fisher, co-star of *Star Wars*, the epic product of Coppola's partner, George Lucas.

AWAKENINGS:
The ubiquitous Robert De Niro plays a more vulnerable hero in *Awakenings*. Co-star Robin Williams plays the doctor who brings De Niro out of a trance to which he inevitably returns.

DANCES WITH WOLVES:
Kevin Costner, an army officer left alone on the

Western frontier, forms a warm relationship with the Indians. Costner glorifies the tribal Indians who Marlon Brando also tried to defend when refusing his Oscar.

DICK TRACY:
For this film, the most memorable part of crime and punishment is the primary colors right off the comics page. Warren Beatty, once in the running for the role of Michael Corleone, played the stolid detective. Al Pacino, who actually got the role of Michael, played Big Boy Caprice.

AVALON:
Also focused on the interaction of families, *Avalon* studies their antagonisms and compassions. This film gently recalls director Barry Levinson's family in the city of Baltimore.

THE HUNT FOR RED OCTOBER:
It's always a pleasure to watch Sean Connery when he isn't playing James Bond —and when he *is*. No one is stealing anything as prosaic as money in *The Hunt for Red October*. They are stealing a nuclear submarine in the movie version of the Tom Clancy bestseller.

CHAPTER 23

The Directors

Francis Coppola was not the first director to turn his attention to crime, adventure, and violence. John Huston and Alfred Hitchcock had also brought violence, menace, malice, and wit to the screen. Francis Coppola is very much in their tradition, and it is instructive to examine the films in which Huston and Hitchcock dealt with the subject that captured Coppola's attention in *The Godfather.* Coppola's brilliant work compares well with the best crime films produced during the Golden Age of Hollywood. When one recalls that he was only thirty-two when he created *The Godfather* and that it became one of the screen's biggest box-office champions, his gifts must be viewed as awesome.

It is also interesting to reflect on Coppola's major contemporaries and how they approached the subject of crime. No man is an island, and this familiar truth applies to directors. For all the leading ones have influenced, and been influenced by, the work of their peers and those who went before them.

Alfred Hitchcock

Like Francis Coppola, Hitchcock shows an alarming variability in his work. Hitchcock had his *Torn Curtain* and Coppola had his *One From the Heart;* Hitchcock had his *Lifeboat* and Coppola had his *Hammett.* In several Hitchcock films, the whole narrative structure was disfigured and distorted. But the value of Hitchcock's finest works, *North by Northwest, Rear Window, Psycho,* and *The Birds,* eclipse these miscalculated works, just as the value of the *Godfather* films and *Apocalypse Now* eclipses *Rumble Fish* and *Tucker.*

Alfred Hitchcock created unmatched tension in crime films.

John Huston

Huston was a charismatic man whose productions were often created amidst creative tempest. To read Lillian Ross' book *Picture,* on the making of *The Red Badge of Courage,* is to see in John Huston the same bold obduracy that Coppola displayed in the teeth of studio restriction. Both men have shown the same daring and enterprise. Huston was flamboyant, theatrical, emotional, as is Coppola. Huston was fortunate in laying hands on such a rich crime novel as Dashiell Hammett's *The Maltese Falcon,* and Coppola was fortunate in finding a novelistic treasure trove like *The Godfather.* The books made a great debut for Huston and a great film for Coppola. Both novels presented their respective directors with a workable cornucopia of incidents. Each director used his story-telling gifts to make a superlative film, and each cast his film well. Huston had the advantages of the Warner Brothers stock company (Bogart, Lorre, Elisha Cook) while Coppola had to reach out to off-Broadway and Tahiti for Pacino and Brando and fight for his choices.

Stanley Kubrick

Critics and audiences accused Kubrick of an excess of explicit brutality in *A Clockwork Orange,* as critics and audiences taxed Coppola with excessive violence in *The Godfather.* It is the dire lesson of *A Clockwork Orange* that watching violence in films has a profound effect

John Huston directed the crime classic *The Maltese Falcon.*

Stanley Kubrick, like Coppola, was accused of excessive violence in *A Clockwork Orange.*

William Friedkin proved expert with a story of cops and crime in *The French Connection*.

Sidney Lumet used Al Pacino effectively in two crime films, *Serpico* and *Dog Day Afternoon*.

on the watcher. *The Godfather* provoked censors on the religious right who claimed that violence in films validated it in our streets.

William Friedkin

Like *The Godfather,* Billy Friedkin's *The French Connection* is the story of crime that prominently features a policeman whose character is wanting—Gene Hackman in *Connection* and Sterling Hayden in *Godfather*. (Coppola cast Hackman in one of his best roles in *The Conversation,* and Friedkin used Coppola's discovery, Al Pacino, in *Cruising*.) Like *The*

Godfather, Connection is not always a paragon of pace. There was one more parallel: in *Godfather,* Coppola observed the seeming paradox that brutal gangsters could be devoted to their families. In *The French Connection,* Friedkin observed that the brutal gangster could be exceedingly well-mannered.

Sidney Lumet

When Francis Coppola re-mixed the first two *Godfather* films in chronological order for NBC, a striking oversight emerged. Whereas Brando and De Niro won Oscars for

their fine performances, Al Pacino had gone unrewarded. Yet his is the presence that dominated the films. It is he who makes the poison of vengeance persuasive. It is he, the lethal hero, who offers a texture of self-pity that seems to justify the murders. But if Pacino received no Oscar, he was rewarded by starring roles in two other crime films directed by Sidney Lumet, *Serpico* and *Dog Day Afternoon*. Interestingly, Sidney Lumet presided over the film version of Agatha Christie's *Murder on the Orient Express,* the film

Clint Eastwood sometimes directed his immensely successful *Dirty Harry* films.

Stephen Spielberg is the master of the action film.

which won Ingrid Bergman the Oscar that Talia Shire aspired to for her work in *Godfather, Part II.* Thus Shire became the only member of the Coppola clan who did not win the Oscar for which she had been nominated.

Clint Eastwood

Clint Eastwood's Dirty Harry films, some of which he directed himself, have proven almost as popular as the *Godfather* trilogy. Like the films of John Wayne and the *Death Wish* series of Charles Bronson, the thesis of Eastwood's Dirty Harry movies is starkly conservative. It takes the view that cops and courts pamper criminals who deserve summary execution. *The Godfather* takes a more tolerant view of the underworld, at least those members who bear the Corleone name. Whereas Coppola was criticized for glorifying gangsters, Eastwood was lauded for executing them.

Steven Spielberg

There are no motorized sharks in *The Godfather.* Coppola is a mechanic of mood and character. He seems to have little interest in cars, unless someone is putting their feet through the windshield. There are no rolling boulders in Staten Island, Lake Tahoe, or

Havana. Spielberg created in *Close Encounters* some of the most elaborate special effects ever assembled. Coppola has little interest in such effects. *Close Encounters* is a high-tech marvel; it is like a mystical experience. There is nothing very mystical about *The Godfather*. Yet there is fellow feeling in Coppola's and Spielberg's attitude toward the fallibility of government. Spielberg is saying that a man should never trust the official version. Coppola is saying that a man should trust his Godfather, not his government.

Robert Altman

Altman's most successful film is *M★A★S★H,* based on a bestseller about the brutality of war. Coppola's most successful film is *The Godfather,* based on a bestseller about the brutality of crime. Elliott Gould and Donald Sutherland brought an improvisational skill to army surgeons that Marlon Brando brought to the role of a Mafia chief. The violence of war and crime produced similar outpourings of gore. But in both cases— war and crime—Hollywood adds a glory to the subject that many consider misplaced.

Bob Rafelson

The film *Five Easy Pieces,* in which Bob Rafelson directed his friend Jack Nicholson,

Robert Altman's *M★A★S★H* was as bloody as *The Godfather.*

Bob Rafelson probed the quirky criminal mind in *Black Widow* and *The Postman Always Rings Twice.*

focuses our attention on an unusual family, the sort one doesn't often encounter on the screen. Early in the film, an outcast son returns home to a family that has very different goals from his own.

And in *The Godfather,* a son returns home to a family of whose methods he disapproves. In a more recent film, *Black Widow,* Rafelson, like Coppola, brings a high style to the art of murder.

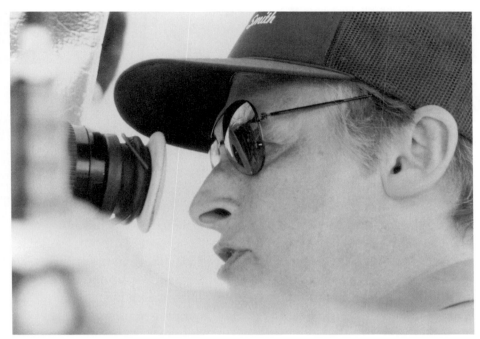

Mike Nichols dealt with emotional violence in *Who's Afraid of Virginia Woolf?*

Mel Brooks has yet to do a send-up of the gangster film.

Mike Nichols

Nichols, who used to create inspired whimsy with actress/director Elaine May, looked to other sources, on the stage and in books, as the source of his best films: *Who's Afraid of Virginia Woolf?* is a riveting play by Edward Albee about verbal violence; *Catch-22* is a classic anti-war novel; *The Graduate* is a delightful book about sex and maturation. ("Mrs. Robinson, you're trying to seduce me.") The graduate in *The Godfather* bears absolutely no resemblance to the graduate in *The Graduate* (except that both Al Pacino and Dustin Hoffman are in the Brando /Actors Studio tradition). And the lunacy of war as pictured in *Catch-22* is surreal compared to the reality of criminal violence in *The Godfather*. And while *Catch-22* is deadpan and cold, *The Godfather* is seething and hot.

Mel Brooks

When Mel Brooks deals with the subject of murder, it comes out frantic and hilarious. *High Anxiety,* his homage to Hitchcock's *Spellbound,* is a delicious romp that stars Cloris Leachman, Harvey Korman, and Brooks himself in the Gregory Peck role. What murders and violence occur make us giggle rather than cringe. There is one memorable sequence when the director sings a love song in the manner of Frank Sinatra, as Al Martino does in the wedding scene of *The Godfather*. Brooks has never done a send-up of *The Godfather* or any gangster film, one of the few genres that has escaped his inspired attention. One wonders what fun Mel Brooks would have with the Corleone family. After all, Brando himself has parodied the Godfather role in the movie *The Freshman.*

CHAPTER 24

The Coppola Family

Hollywood has always been a land of dynasties. The literary Mankiewiczes—Joe, Herman, Don and Tom—wrote some of the most distinguished screenplays you can name, from *Citizen Kane* to *All About Eve*. The acting Barrymores included John, Ethel, and Lionel. More recent acting dynasties include Lloyd Bridges and sons; Martin Sheen and sons; Kirk Douglas and son; the Quaid brothers; and the Bottoms brothers. Among the moguls of yore were the Warner brothers, the Cohn brothers, Louis B. Mayer and David Selznick, who proved the son-in-law also rises; B. P. Schulberg and son Budd; Darryl Zanuck and son; Sam Goldwyn and son; Carl Laemmle and his assorted kin on the Universal lot. The Coppola family continue this tradition as one of Tinseltown's most successful, visible, obstreperous families: writer/director/producer Francis, composer/arranger Carmine, actress Talia, and ingenue Sofia.

But Francis Coppola has more in common with the old studio dynasties than mere family. He has the same vibrant self-confidence, the same willingness to take a risk, the same Barnumesque addiction to show biz. Thanks to Francis, we have heard much of the Corleone family; but the Coppola family holds as great an interest. No other recent Hollywood dynasty has combined and recombined so often in productive filmmaking.

———

A visit to Bellagio Road in Bel Air will reveal the Casa Coppola, the house where Francis Coppola lives with his artist wife Eleanor, his sister Talia Shire, and her producer husband Jack Schwartzman. Several seasons back, Talia and Jack produced a James Bond thriller, *Never Say Never Again*. It is a title that applied well to her brother Francis' strategy of success. If he ever said "never again" to a *Godfather* sequel, he twice recanted.

———

In making the original *Godfather*, Francis had invested the film with his own strong emotions about family allegiance. He adorned it with all he recalled of coming-of-age in a fiercely loyal Italian-American clan. Godfatherphiles recall the frequent occasions in the films where a member of the family is reminded of the duties of family members. After Sonny speaks out at a meeting of the Five Families, his father admonishes him to never let anyone outside the family know what he is thinking. On a visit to Vegas, Michael admonishes his brother Fredo, "Don't ever take sides with anyone against the family." It is a recurring motif, this theme of familial loyalty. It may explain the film's singular appeal: despite the barbarity of the way the Corleones settle disputes, they possess a family cohesion that, in the age of the "nuclear family," we want to emulate. The family that slays together, stays together.

———

All of the *Godfather* films delineate the feelings and happenings of the Coppola family. *The Godfather* paints a picture of family structure and sequence. As Talia describes it, "This brother is

Francis' sister, Talia Shire

first, this one is second, the girl Connie is screwed up until the mother dies. There's some of that in our family and some of that in all Italian families. . . ."

The production of *Godfather II* was a time of relative contentment in the Coppola clan, more so than during the filming of the original *Godfather*. This was because Francis wielded more power in the second production, and power bred security and tranquility. The second time around, he felt no trepidation about using family members in the movie; he felt more insulated to criticism. During *The Godfather* he was hesitant about having his family on board. Later, he had no such hesitation.

■■■■■

Godfather II fostered Talia's career. True, Ingrid Bergman had won the Oscar that Talia coveted. But something of inestimable value flowed from the film. An ambitious young screenwriter/actor named Sylvester Stallone had sent his script for a boxing movie to her husband, composer David Shire. Though Shire passed on the project, Talia saw herself in the role of the shy girlfriend. She read for the role and got it. Talia became Adrian, the

diffident pet store employee in *Rocky,* living with her brutish brother, Burt Young. "Adrian was me," said Talia, "that whole syndrome: 'Please God, don't notice me but won't somebody notice me?' "

■■■■■

The unprecedented dual success of *Godfather I* and *II* brought a flush of fame to the Coppola family that was not an unqualified benediction. Said mother Italia, "I feel about this fame that if it didn't happen I would have loved it. We are less happy. I hate fame. . . . And the relatives have broken my heart. . . . They push everybody away to get to Francis."

■■■■■

It is in the nature of life— and Hollywood life, in particular—that it has its peaks and valleys; audiences are fickle and uninterrupted success is an oxymoron. Francis was wounded when he lost the Academy Award he had wanted for *Apocalypse Now* to *Kramer vs. Kramer.*

Concurrently, his sister's career went into a slide. She appeared in three movies that came and went, *Old Boyfriends, Prophecy,* and *Windows.* They moved rapidly from obscurity to

oblivion. Simultaneously, her union with David Shire was coming unglued.

■■■■■

Groucho Marx said that nothing is as pleasing as the sound of grinding bones. Some in Hollywood welcome the failure of others and deride their successes. Some reproached the Coppolas for showing favoritism within the family. Yet their careers were bound together by love and talent. Members of some Hollywood clans avoid making films together, seeking independence; the Coppolas relished togetherness. Perhaps it was due to the Italian tradition of family fealty and obligation that the Coppola's continued working together. Here is the list of family members in each of the *Godfather* movies:

COPPOLAS IN *THE GODFATHER*

Francis directed and co-wrote the screenplay.
Talia, his sister, played Connie Corleone.
Carmine, his father, can be observed pounding the piano in the scene where Corleone soldiers prepare for battle.

Francis' daughter, Sofia Coppola

Carmine conducted the orchestra for the wedding scene and wrote incidental music for the film.

Carmine and Italia, Francis' father and mother, can be seen dining at the Italian restaurant where Michael murders McCluskey and Sollozzo.

Sofia, Francis' daughter, played Connie's son at the baptism. She was about three weeks old.

August, Francis' brother, served as script consultant.

Gian-Carlo, Francis' elder son, was an extra in the baptism scene. So was *Roman,* Francis' younger son, and *Eleanor,* Francis' wife.

Francis' father, composer/conductor Carmine Coppola

COPPOLAS IN *GODFATHER, PART II*

Francis directed, produced, and co-wrote the screenplay.

Talia reprised the role of Connie.

The drawing left by Michael's son, Anthony, on his dad's pillow was actually drawn by Coppola's son, Gian-Carlo, for his dad.

Italia was told by her son that he would use her in the death scene when Morgana King refused to lay in an open casket.

Eleanor, Gian-Carlo, Roman, and *Sofia* were all extras.

Carmine co-composed the musical score with Nino Rota.

Francisco Pennino, Francis' grandfather, wrote the musical that is attended by De Niro at which he sees Fanucci. It was translated by Francis' mother.

COPPOLAS IN *GODFATHER, PART III*

Sofia played Michael's daughter, Mary.

Talia again reprised Connie Corleone.

Carmine composed the score and did a cameo as a bandleader.

Italia was an extra.

Anton, Francis' uncle and Carmine's brother, conducted the opera orchestra in Sicily.

CHAPTER 25

By the Numbers

6 months	Approximate shooting time of *Godfather I*.
6 months	Approximate shooting time of *Godfather II*.
7 weeks	Number of weeks behind schedule of *Godfather III*.
11 percent	Percentage over budget on *Godfather III*.
$51 million	Budget of *Godfather III*.
$75 million	Estimated cost to produce and promote *Godfather III*.
67 weeks	How long *The Godfather* novel was on the bestseller list.
163 pages	Number of pages of shooting script of *The Godfather,* versus the usual 120 pages.
6 weeks	How long Brando worked on *The Godfather*.
3 Oscars	How many *The Godfather* won.
32	How old Coppola was when he made *The Godfather*.
16	How many hugs, kisses, and squeezes occur in *The Godfather*.
5	Number of counts of perjury Michael faced.
50	Number of scenes in the original *Godfather* script.
150	Number of extras used for Don's funeral.
20	Number of limos used for Don's funeral.
$12,000	Cost of flowers and wreaths in funeral scene.
$4,000	Cost of an average hour of filming.
$5,000	Rent of the Coppola/Ruddy offices located at Filmways Studios.

$80,000	Cost of the set of Don's house, built in Hoboken, N.J.
$75,000	Prop budget in *The Godfather*.
$1 million	Original budget of *The Godfather*.
$6.2 million	Actual budget of *The Godfather*.
80	Number of days Coppola requested to shoot *The Godfather*.
83	Number of days he was given.
77	Number of days it took.
500,000	Number of feet of film printed for *The Godfather*.
90	Number of hours of film printed.
30 to 1	Ratio of film footage shot to film footage used.
$150,000	Cost of the French-language dub.
$454,000	Grossed by *The Godfather* in the five N.Y. theaters in the first week.
$8 million	Grossed by *The Godfather* in 365 theaters in the first week.
$6 million	Grossed in the second week.
$5 million	Grossed in the third week.
$3 million	Grossed in each of the next four weeks.
$2 million	Grossed for twenty-three consecutive weeks.
$72,900,000	The top film gross, for *Gone With the Wind*, until *The Godfather*.
$68,400,000	Grossed by *The Sound of Music*.
$81,500,000	Returned to Paramount in rentals after *The Godfather's* first year.
$150 million	Estimated worldwide gross of *The Godfather*.
132 million	People had seen the film by January 1975.
$1.50 adults	Ticket price on military installations.

$.75	Usual ticket price on military installations.
$5,000	Advance Puzo received from his publishers, G.P. Putnam's Sons.
$410,000	Advance Puzo received for paperback rights to *The Godfather*.
$2.5 million	Amount Putnam received in royalties on paperback sales.
100	Number of completed pages of novel when Puzo made deal with Paramount optioning movie rights.
$12,000	Amount paid by Paramount to option movie rights.
$50,000	Additional sum Puzo was paid when Paramount exercised the option to make the film.
$80,000	Total amount of an escalator clause for Puzo from Paramount.
$100,000	Additional sum paid by Paramount to Puzo for writing screenplay with Coppola.
2.5 percent	Coppola's participation in net rentals.
$7 million	Coppola earned this amount from *Godfather* and *Godfather, Part II*.
$175,000	Coppola's fee for co-writing and directing *The Godfather*.
$1,500	Per diem expenses received by Coppola.
$500	Weekly expenses received by Puzo.
$1,000	Weekly expenses received by Brando.
$125,000 plus 10 percent	Deal Coppola turned down which would have given him less up-front but more back-end.
$4 million	Amount Coppola lost by this decision.
$50,000	Sum received by Brando for his six weeks' work.
$1.5 million	Ceiling of Brando's earnings.
$300,000	According to Peter Bart, amount Brando received, since he sold his points back to the studio.

5 percent	Amount of the film that Brando owned.
$35,000	Total sum received by Al Pacino.
$35,000	Total sum received by James Caan.
$35,000	Total sum received by Diane Keaton.
$36,000	Amount received by Robert Duvall for eight weeks' work.
20 percent	Amount that actors' salaries comprised in *The Godfather* budget.
$38 a share	The figure at which Gulf + Western stock closed on the day *Godfather* premiered.
$44.25 a share	The figure at which the stock closed the next day.
$45,000	Value of the Mercedes Benz given to Coppola for creating most successful film in history.
2 hours, 56 minutes	Length of *The Godfather*.
$10 million	Amount NBC paid Paramount for two-night single airing of *The Godfather*.
$750,000	Amount networks normally paid studios for successful films.
$510,000	Sum Coppola received to edit the film for television.
$250,000 a minute	Amount NBC charged advertisers for each of twenty-eight commercial minutes.
$215,000 a minute	Amount network charged advertisers for Super Bowl.
90 million	Number of viewers who watched *The Godfather*.
38 percent	Portion of people with sets on who were watching *The Godfather*.
6.5 million	Number of people in New York who watched first half of *The Godfather*.
7 million	Number of people in New York who watched concluding part of *The Godfather*.
1.5 million	Number of New Yorkers who normally watch "Monday Night Football."
20–25 percent	How far business was off at Elaine's restaurant during *The Godfather* airing.

3 hours, 30 minutes	The length of *Godfather II*.
$27 million	Sum Paramount received in advance rental guarantees for *Godfather II* from 340 theaters.
$29 million	Amount *Godfather II* racked up in domestic rentals by end of 1975. (It opened December 1974.)
$175,000	Amount Puzo received to write script of *Godfather II* with Coppola.
$1 million	Amount Coppola received to write, direct and produce *Godfather II*.
13 percent	Gross Coppola received, plus salary, which amounted to three to four million dollars.
$500,000	Pacino's salary for *Godfather II,* plus 10 percent of the gross after break-even.
$10,000	Amount Lee Strasberg was offered and rejected.
$30,000	Amount Lee Strasberg accepted.
$58,000	Amount Lee Strasberg received due to delays and overtime.
16 years	Time elapsed between release of *Godfather II* and *III*.
20 pages	How much Coppola cut from script to save money on *Godfather III*.
12	Number of versions of *Godfather III* that were commissioned by Paramount.
675,000 feet	Film shot for *Godfather III*.
285,000 feet	Film printed for *Godfather III*.
30 to 1	Ratio of film shot to film used on *Godfather III*.
$2 million	Cost of shooting two weeks of additional footage for *Godfather III*.
$5 million	Amount received by Al Pacino for his role of Michael in *Godfather III*.
$800 million	Amount *Godfather I* and *II* brought in since 1972 in theatrical, television, video, and licensing.

Adam, Christina. *Moving Image,* January 1982. "Interning with the Godfather."

Ames, Katrine, with William J. Cook. *Newsweek,* July 21, 1975. "*Godfather III.*"

Babitz, Eve. *Coast,* April 1975. "Francis Ford Coppola."

Beck, Marilyn, Syndicated column. *Los Angeles Herald Examiner,* June 14, 1983. "Tough Harmonies."

Biskind, Peter. *The Godfather Companion.* Harper Perennial, New York, 1990.

Boyer, Peter. *Vanity Fair,* June 1990. "Under the Gun."

Boyum, Joy Gould. *Wall Street Journal,* December 23, 1974. "More Deaths in the Family."

Broeske, Pat H. *Los Angeles Times,* December 25, 1990. "Mixed Reviews for Coppola's *Godfather III.*"

Byrge, Duane. *Press-Telegram,* December 21, 1990. "Bravos & Blood."

Byron, Stuart. *New York,* July 17, 1978. "The War of the Movie Critics."

Cage, Nicholas. *New York Times,* March 19, 1972. "A Few Family Murders."

Campbell, William. *Interview,* November 1988.

Canby, Vincent, *The New York Times:*
March 12, 1972. "Bravo Brando's Godfather;" April 8, 1972. "How Do You Top *Godfather?*"; December 13, 1974. "*Godfather, Part II* Is Hard to Define." December 22, 1974. "*The Godfather, Part II*: One Godfather Too Many."

Carroll, Jon. *New York,* November 13, 1974. "Coppola: Bringing in the Next Godfather."

Chaillet, Jean-Paul and Elizabeth Vincent. *Francis Ford Coppola.* St. Martin's Press, New York, 1984.

Cocks, Jay. *Time,* April 3, 1972. "The Godsons."

Coppola, Eleanor. *Vogue,* December 1990. "The Godfather Diary."

Corliss, Richard. *Time,* December 24, 1990. "Schemes and Dreams for Christmas."

Cowie, Peter. *Connoisseur,* December 1990. "The Whole Godfather."

Cowie, Peter. *Coppola: A Biography.* Scribner's, New York, 1990.

Cowie, Peter. *Daily Variety,* January 4, 1990. "Coppola Making $44 Mil *Godfather 3* For Paramount 'His Way'."

Cowie, Peter. *The Sunday Times* (London), January 14, 1990. "An Offer Coppola Couldn't Refuse."

Davis, Ivor and Sally Ogle. *Los Angeles,* December 1990. "It Ain't Over Till the Fat Man Directs."

Easton, Nina J. *Los Angeles Times,* December 25, 1990. "Paramount's Epic *Godfather III* Struggle."

Farber, Stephen. *Sight and Sound,* Autumn 1972. "Coppola and *The Godfather.*"

Ginnane, Antony and David Stratton. *Cinema Papers,* November-December 1975. "Francis Ford Coppola."

Godfather II. Press booklet. Paramount Pictures, 1975.

Goodwin, Michael and Naomi Wise. *On The Edge: The Life and Times of Francis Coppola.* William Morrow, New York, 1989.

Harrison, Barbara Grizzuti. *Life,* November 1990. "*Godfather III.*"

Haskell, Molly. *Village Voice,* April 19, 1975. "The Corleone Saga Sags."

Hoberman, J. *Village Voice,* December 25, 1990. "Like Godfather."

Hollywood Reporter, newsbriefs, April 11, 1975. Coppola discusses *Godfather II* as an art film.

Honeycutt, Kirk. *Los Angeles Daily News,* April 15, 1983. "Francis Coppola Drifts Away from His Talent." Career analysis of Godfather et al.

Kael, Pauline. *The New Yorker,* film reviews:
  March 18, 1972. *The Godfather;* December 23, 1974. *Godfather II;* January 14, 1991. *Godfather III.*

Kauffman, Stanley. *New Republic,* April 1, 1972. Review of *The Godfather;* January 18, 1975. Review of *Godfather II;* January 21, 1991. Review of *Godfather III.*

Kroll, Jack. *Newsweek,* May 28, 1990. "The Offer He Didn't Refuse;" December 24, 1990. "The Corleones Return."

Ladies Home Journal, June 1972. "The Story Behind *The Godfather* by the Men Who Lived It."

Landro, Laura. *Wall Street Journal,* February 9, 1990. "*Godfather III* Filming Begins After 15 Years and 3 Studio Regimes;" December 11, 1990. "Paramount in the Dark Before the Don."

Lichtenstein, Grace. *New York Times,* March 20, 1971. "Godfather Film Won't Mention Mafia."

Maslin, Janet. *New York Times,* December 25, 1990. "The Corleones Try to Go Straight in *The Godfather, Part III.*"

Mathews, Jack. *Los Angeles Times,* January 13, 1991. "Declining Expectations."

McBride, Joseph. *American Film,* November 1975. "Coppola Inc." *Film Makers on Film Making, Vol. 2.* J. P. Tarcher, Los Angeles, 1983.

Mermelstein, David. *Village View,* December 28, 1990. "An Offer You Can't Refuse."

Moss, Marilyn. *Boxoffice,* October 1990. "*The Godfather, Part III*—Recapturing the Myth."

Mottley, Bob. *New Times,* May 3, 1974. "Two Godfathers."

Murray, William. *Playboy,* July 1975. "Playboy Interview: Francis Ford Coppola."

New York magazine:
  April 16, 1972. "Profits of *The Godfather;*" April 26, 1972. *"Notes on People."* Visiting Soviets discuss *The Godfather;* October 13, 1972. "Sicily Gets Hollywood Version of the Godfather;" January 7, 1991. "The Grandfather."

Orth, Maureen. *Newsweek,* November 25, 1974. "The New Hollywood—Godfather of the Movies."

Playboy, June, 1972. Review of *The Godfather, Part II.*

Powers, John. *L.A. Weekly,* December 28, 1990. "Quiet Flows the Don."

Rockwell, John. *The Saturday Review,* December 2, 1972. "My Own Little City, My Own Little Opera."

Rohter, Larry. *New York Times,* December 23, 1990. "Francis Ford Coppola Couldn't Refuse This Offer."

Rosen, Marjorie. *Film Comment,* July 1974. "Francis Ford Coppola."

Ruddy, Al. *Interview,* October 1988. Deals and production of *The Godfather.*

Salamon, Julie. *Wall Street Journal,* December 27, 1990. "Film: Al Pacino as a Repentant Godfather."

Sarris, Andrew. *Village Voice,* film reviews, March 16, March 23, 1972. *The Godfather.*

Schlesinger, Arthur, Jr. *Vogue,* May 1972. "*The Godfather* Plays on Secret Admiration for Men Who Get What They Want."

Schickel, Richard. *Brando, A Life in Our Times.* Atheneum, New York, 1991.

Sheehan, Henry. *Reader,* December 21, 1990. "*Godfather III*: The Work of a Master."

Short, Martin. *Stills,* March 1986. "The Mob and the Movies."

Simon, John. *New York,* March 31, 1975. "Films" review.

Sorel, Edward. *Esquire,* August 1981. "Movie Classics: *The Godfather.*"

Sragow, Michael. *Squire,* October 1990. "Why We're Married to the Mob."

Tatara, Paul. *US,* November 12, 1990. "On the Set: Mob Control."

Variety, Daily:

February 3, 1971. Brando cast as Don Corleone; February 24, 1971. *Godfather* preproduction problems; January 26, 1972. "Coppola Directs Private Lives;" October 1, 1973. *Godfather II* starts shooting; February 6, 1974. Pacino gets pneumonia; June 19, 1974. "God II Completes 8 Months of Photography;" July 31, 1974. "An NBC-TV Offer Par Couldn't Refuse"; December 18, 1974. *Godfather II* personnel payments; February 26, 1975. *Godfather II* Oscar nominations; March 19, 1975. *Godfather II* DG award; April 16, 1975. Oscars awarded; May 4, 1983. New analysis of all-time box office champs; August 5, 1988. Possible *Godfather III.*

Walker, Alexander. *Evening Standard* (London), December 20, 1990. "God Against the Mob."

Wall Street Journal, April 4, 1974. "Coming Attractions." An editorial.

Weekly Variety, news stories:

September 30, 1970. "Coppola-Par Tie;" October 14, 1970. "Coppola Fighing Ruddy Re Gotham;" February 3, 1971. "That Unknown Face: It's Marlon Brando;" February 17, 1971. "Make-Believe Picket Paramount;" February 24, 1971. "Hollywood Sound Track."

GERALD GARDNER has written over 25 books on the entertainment world and the American presidency. The former include *The Censorship Papers, I Coulda Been a Contender,* and *The Way I Was* (with Marvin Hamlisch). His political books include *All the Presidents' Wits, The Mocking of the President, Robert Kennedy in New York,* and the bestselling *Who's In Charge Here?* series. He has written several motion pictures and helped create such TV shows as "That Was the Week That Was," "Get Smart," and "The Monkees." Gardner lectures widely on the history of film censorship and on presidential humor. He has contributed wit to the speeches of John and Robert Kennedy.

HARRIET MODELL GARDNER is co-author of *Pictorial History of Gone With the Wind* (originally published as *The Tara Treasury),* which was a Literary Guild Selection. She also wrote the nationally syndicated column "Almanac." Her work has appeared in various magazines. The Gardners live in Beverly Hills.